**Help us preserve
our collection.
Report damage at
Circulation Desk.**

**You are
responsible for
materials borrowed
on your card.**

Withdrawn

DEMCO

A WRITER'S REALITY

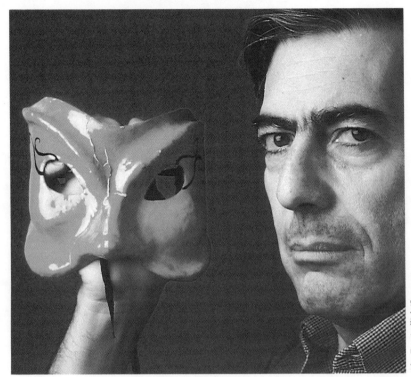

Mario Vargas Llosa

MARIO VARGAS LLOSA | A Writer's Reality

Edited, with an introduction by
Myron I. Lichtblau

SYRACUSE UNIVERSITY PRESS

First Edition 1991
  91 92 93 94 95 96 97 98 99   6 5 4 3 2 1
            /20792 Online
The paper used in this publication meets the minimum requirements of American
National Standard for Information Sciences — Permanence of Paper for Printed
Library Materials, ANSI Z39.48-1984. ∞™

Library of Congress Cataloging-in-Publication Data

Vargas Llosa, Mario, 1936–
      A writer's reality / Mario Vargas Llosa ; edited with an introduction
  by Myron I. Lichtblau. — 1st ed.
            p. cm.
      Based on lectures given by the author at Syracuse University in Mar. and
  Apr. 1988.
      Includes index.
      ISBN 0-8156-0253-7 (alk. paper)
      1. Vargas Llosa, Mario, 1936–   . 2. Authorship.   I. Lichtblau,
  Myron I., 1925–   . II. Title.
  PQ8498.32.A65A5   1990
  863 — dc20   90-43036
                                                                                    CIP

Manufactured in the United States of America

The origin of this book is the series of lectures that Mario Vargas Llosa delivered, in English, at Syracuse University during his time as the Jeannette K. Watson Distinguished Visiting Professor in the Humanities in March and April 1988.

M.I.L.

MARIO VARGAS LLOSA, Peruvian novelist and short-story writer, has established himself as one of the most important of contemporary writers in the Spanish language. Part of the generation of novelists emerging in the 1950s that put Hispanic American fiction in the forefront of world letters, Vargas Llosa's work has been nominated several times for the Nobel Prize. While his novels deal with Peruvian culture, the problems that he addresses are a universal metaphor for the human condition. Among his many books are *The Time of the Hero, Conversation in The Cathedral, Aunt Julia and the Scriptwriter,* and *The Real Life of Alejandro Mayta.*

MYRON I. LICHTBLAU is Professor of Latin American Literature at Syracuse University. He is the author of *Manuel Gálvez* and the translator of Eduardo Mallea's *History of an Argentine Passion.*

Contents

Introduction

Myron I. Lichtblau

Mario Vargas Llosa belongs to that select group of highly gifted writers of the so-called boom generation that catapulted Latin American fiction to the forefront of world literature. Along with Jorge Luis Borges, Gabriel García Márquez, and Carlos Fuentes, the Peruvian novelist disengaged fiction writing in Latin America from its regionalism and sociological orientation and made it a vehicle for the expression of more universal, human values within the context of the American experience. Born in 1936, Vargas Llosa has had a remarkable career as journalist, politician, essayist, dramatist, short story writer, and most importantly, as a serious, committed novelist whose works have been enthusiastically acclaimed by both professional critics and the general reading public.

Few writers are as candid about their work as Vargas Llosa; even fewer are as perceptive. His directness and candor concerning those elements of his life that bear significantly on his novels illuminate his literary personality and reveal his abiding concerns about fiction writing in general and his own art in particular. In his writings and public lectures, such as those comprising this volume, Vargas Llosa is not only articulate and insightful about the complicated process of novelistic creation that obtains when he sets out to write a work of fiction but is extremely conscious as well of the genesis of each work, the source of inspiration, and the myriad environmental and psychological forces that play on his mind and emotions as that process is evolving.

The essence of Vargas Llosa's art is personal experience turned fiction. It is for this reason that he speaks so constantly about people, books, and events in his life, for they form the wellspring of many of his best fictional works. The conversion of what Vargas Llosa calls real reality to a fictional reality is as complete and convincing as the mimetic reproduction of external reality in the hands of more traditional writers of past generations. But it is far more artistic and aesthetically pleasing. Whether in *The Time of the Hero, The Green House,* or *Aunt Julia and the Scriptwriter,* the transmutation of experiential reality to fiction is accomplished through the novelist's imaginative manipulation of time sequences, spatial correspondences, narrative structures, and even ontological systems.

It is thus not so much the transformation of reality that the reader senses as the remaking of the order and the position in which common elements of human experience occur and coalesce. The recording of simultaneous but different actions in the same narrative space, the concept of the *vasos comunicantes,* in which two dialogues spatially and temporally independent are interwoven into one, the running together of thought processes in the form of interior monologues and stream of consciousness, and the fragmenting or refracting of everyday occurrences — these are some of the techniques that change one level of reality into another, that help create one reality out of another, that invent a new reality and invite the reader to be part of it.

Vargas Llosa's genius showed itself early, in his first novel, published in 1962 when he was twenty-six years old. A seemingly autobiographical work about the novelist's adolescent years in the Leoncio Prado Military Academy, *The Time of the Hero* amazed most critics because of its mastery of novelistic technique and its sensitive treatment of difficult thematic material. Essentially a *Bildungsroman,* the novel is the cadets' collective initiation into life, but is at the same time a microcosm of Peruvian society in its variegated and perniciously differentiated strata. The violence, deception, and duplicity that prevail at the academy at all levels within its walls reflect the sham, hypocrisy, and injustices of the outside world and suggest that all attempts to remedy these ills will meet with the fierce resistance of established order and imbedded systems of conduct and control. In their symbolic representation, the actions of the cadets and military officials paint an abject picture of Peruvian life, in which the strict codes of behavior of the various social classes—the military, the bourgeoisie, the middle class—are challenged as being outmoded and incompatible with the needs and aspirations of a changing society.

In *The Green House* (1966), Vargas Llosa's second and perhaps most celebrated novel, the two settings of Piura, a coastal, desert city in the extreme north, and Santa María de Nieva, a tiny trading post in the Amazon region, represent the division of Peru into two separate and distinct cultures. Structurally, the novel is Vargas Llosa's most complex and labyrinthine, as five independent stories are narrated in rotation within each of the four principal sections of the work and the epilogue. The rupture of chronological time, the fragmentation of the thought processes of the characters, and the fortuitous confluence of episodes and lives, all contribute to the kaleidoscopic image of an almost mythical and transcendental reality. With an inordinate control of this vast canvas of narrative material, Vargas Llosa weaves the five stories of frustration and ultimate defeat in environments as inexorable as they are hostile: Fushía, the Japanese-Peruvian truculent smuggler who ends his days in a leper colony; the mysterious Anselmo who builds the first brothel on the outskirts of Piura, seduces the blind and mute Antoñita and forces her to live in the same "green house," and then works as a musician in the second bordello built on the ashes of the first by his natural daughter Chunga; the mission of the nuns of Santa María de Nieva to "civilize" and educate the Aguaruna Indian girls, among them Bonifacia; Jum, an Aguaruna chief who is horribly tortured because he opposes the exploitation of his people by the avaricious *patrones;* and finally the "Invincibles," a rowdy gang of young toughs from the slums of La Mangachería. The "green house" itself touches the lives of several important characters in the novel and for some critics represents a powerful symbol of the Spanish conquest and colonial rule, of the destruction of flourishing Indian civilizations, and the degradation of their inhabitants. In Vargas Llosa's essay on the early chronicle, the novelist cogently synthesizes the fundamental nature of Peruvian civilization, words which may well apply to one of the basic themes of *The Green House:* "Two cultures, one Western and modern, the other aboriginal and archaic, badly coexist, separated from each other because of the exploitation and discrimination that the former exercises over the latter."

In his next novel, *Conversation in The Cathedral* (1969), Vargas Llosa portrays the social and political atmosphere in Peru during the regime of Manuel Odría, 1948–56, a corrupt dictatorship that the novelist lived through as a university student in Lima. Again, violence, sham, chicanery, and fear are the central motifs in this disturbing novel set principally in Lima but with many episodes situated in other regions of the country, from the coastal sections to the Andes. "The Cathedral" is a cafe and bar in the capital, a popular gathering place to talk, discuss, and recollect. The dialogue between the journalist Santiago Zavala and his father's ex-chauffeur Ambrosio Pardo is just the frame, or point of reference, for the more important dialogues that form the interpolated portions of the novel. These dialogues are evoked by the reminiscences of the two characters and involve people and events of the reconstructed past during Odría's term of office. As both men conjure up episodes of fraud and corruption to which their own fathers were witnesses, the sordid picture of Peruvian life is revealed in ironical historical perspective.

Until 1972, when *Captain Pantoja and the Special Service* was published, humor was noticeably absent in Vargas Llosa's novels. For a long time he persisted in the belief that humor and fiction were incompatible. He distrusted humor as an instrument for portraying reality and originally set out to write *Captain Pantoja and the Special Service* in the completely serious vein that had characterized his three previous novels. But Vargas Llosa soon realized not only that the story itself, turning on Captain Pantoja's overly zealous efforts to organize a service that would supply prostitutes to a military garrison in the Amazon, could be told much more effectively if narrated in a comic way but that humor was absolutely necessary for the work to be convincing. Yet underneath the comedic portrayal of Pantoja's dedication and industry, with military officialdom, useless documentation, and red tape standing in ironic contrast to the nature of the assignment, is the impelling picture of bureaucratic efficiency gone wild, of institutionalized assiduousness that warps the mind and distorts reality, of overspecialization that causes men to sacrifice everything for the accomplishment of their tiny mission.

In *Aunt Julia and the Scriptwriter* (1977), two independent stories are narrated in alternate chapters of the novel. Both stories issue from Vargas Llosa's life experiences and become fiction not so much because the novelist changed reality but because he superimposed a different reality on the observable reality, envisaged a new reality on the basis of the old. *Aunt Julia and the Scriptwriter* represents Vargas Llosa at his most ingenious and entertaining best. One story relates Varguitas's courtship and marriage to his Aunt Julia, an aunt by marriage, when he was just eighteen years old and she twelve years older. The other deals with a radio script writer, Pedro Camacho, who writes so many different scripts peopled with so many diverse characters that he has difficulty keeping them all straight and eventually winds up inserting all sorts of inaccuracies and contradictions in the tales to the amazement and annoyance of his radio audience. *Aunt Julia and the Scriptwriter* is a novel about writing, about the act of writing, of writing within writing, as Varguitas is portrayed as a student employed part time at a radio station putting together the news, while his companion at work is Pedro Camacho, who becomes so enmeshed in his own creations that at one point he even dons a disguise for one of his characters. The juxtaposition of these two concurrent narrations—one, the melodramatic soap operas themselves and Camacho's bizarre personality; the other, the equally melodramatic story of Varguitas's youthful romance—produces a fascinating contrapuntal narrative design that is as entertaining as it is pregnant with deep psychological import.

Reality transformed into fiction occurs too in *The War of the End of the World* (1984) and *The Real Life of Alejandro Mayta* (1986), but it is transformation of a different kind of reality, a historical reality in which Vargas Llosa has participated not directly or experientially, but intellectually and emotionally through the power of his own readings. With the irony of historical retrospect, *The War of the End of the World* narrates the rebellion of 1896 against the Republic of Brazil, which had won its independence from Portugal just a few years before. The rebellion in the northeast province of Bahia was headed by Antonio Conselheiro and was finally put down after four bloody military expeditions. Just as Vargas Llosa sees Peru divided into two cultures, so too does he perceive this rebellion as a struggle between westernized, "civilized," Brazil, represented by the military forces and official authorities, and the "primitive" people of the hinterland. What is worse, the only contact between the two cultures is ironically a military encounter.

In *The Real Life of Alejandro Mayta,* the reader tries to reconstruct the past through participants and witnesses to that past, but what results is a blurred, ambiguous fiction within another fiction that recounts past events in accord with individual perspectives and interests. In this case, reality becomes fiction not only because the novelist fictionalized it but because the acts of remembering are so deformed or willfully mendacious that it is itself a fiction. The novel tries to assemble the fragmented pieces of the story of the unsuccessful rebellion in the Peruvian Andes in 1958, led by the leftist Alejandro Mayta. The nature of Vargas Llosa's fictional representation of the insurrection is clearly indicated in the Spanish title *Historia de Alejandro Mayta* because the word *historia* means both history and story, but the English translation of *history* fails to suggest the ironical interplay of truth and nontruth so important to the novel's development.

The versatility of Vargas Llosa's fiction is matched only by its unpredictability. We never quite know what to expect next from the novelist's pen, a point reinforced by the newest of his books, *In Praise of the Stepmother,* billed by his publisher as "an erotic masterpiece," which will appear in the fall of 1990. The appearance in 1987 of *Who Killed Palomino Romero?* apparently invited the reader to the detective novel, to popular fiction, to entertaining but inconsequential literary fare. The reader did get a detective novel, indeed Lieutenant Silva and his assistant Lituma are investigating a baffling homicide, the sadistic murder of an air cadet. But it got much more, an intense study of human relationships at the most fundamental level, and more importantly a study of the social class system and its pernicious effects on those human relationships.

The theme of acculturation, which Vargas Llosa treats tangentially in some novels, becomes a central concern in *The Storyteller* (1988), one of the most problematic of the novelist's works in its cultural and social implications. The novel is a journey to the past, to the civilization of the Machiguengas deep in the Amazon jungle, where tribal practices and religious rites are as out of step with westernized man as westernized man is ignorant and intolerant of their ancient culture. The question is whether "civilized" man has a moral responsibility to impose his culture and set of values on other less-advanced cultures. In *The Storyteller,* a Peruvian university student, Jewish on his father's side, ventures into this unknown world with an almost mystical mission, and not only learns its mores and empathizes with its primitive life-style but totally identifies himself with the natives, who accept him as one of their own and even make him their venerated storyteller.

Vargas Llosas's fiction, in synthesis, tries to answer the question of what happens when two different and separated worlds are placed in confrontation. For Vargas Llosa, Peru is not a monolithic entity, even within the commonality of national borders, and the clash of opposing civilizations and cultures is as intractable in its realization as it is tragic in its consequences. The novelist's reordering of the temporal and spatial structures that inform many of his works is rarely a gratuitous incursion into empirical reality but rather a masterful technique used to abet the process of transforming reality into a fictional vision of reality. This transformation is the core of Vargas Llosa's art and its greatest triumph.

Chronology

<table>
<tr><td>1936</td><td>March 28. Born in Arequipa, Peru, of a long-established family. His parents separated shortly after his birth, and he was raised by his maternal grandparents in Cochabamba, Bolivia.</td></tr>
<tr><td>1941–49</td><td>Receives early schooling in Cochabamba and in Piura, Peru.</td></tr>
<tr><td>1950</td><td>His parents reunited, he attends the Leoncio Prado Military Academy in Lima.</td></tr>
<tr><td>1952</td><td>Writes a play, La huida del Inca (The Flight of the Inca), and has it produced.</td></tr>
<tr><td>1955</td><td>Marries Julia Urquidi, a Bolivian, aunt by marriage.</td></tr>
<tr><td>1956–58</td><td>Works in Lima in a variety of jobs—in broadcasting, in journalism, in the library of the Club Nacional, at the university as a professor's assistant.</td></tr>
<tr><td>1958</td><td>Graduates from the University of San Marcos in Lima with a degree in literature.</td></tr>
<tr><td>1959</td><td>Publishes his first book, Los jefes (The Leaders), a collection of short stories, for which he wins the Leopoldo Alas Prize.</td></tr>
<tr><td>1959</td><td>Enrolls as a doctoral student at the University of Madrid.</td></tr>
</table>

1959   In Paris, works as a translator, interpreter, and broadcaster for Radio-Télévision Française.

1963   Publishes his first novel, *La ciudad y los perros (The Time of the Hero),* a microcosm of Peruvian society based on his adolescent experiences at the Leoncio Prado school.

1964   During a short stay in Peru, travels to the jungle that is the setting for *The Green House.*

1965   Goes to Cuba as a judge for literary awards given by the Casa de las Américas and to show his sympathy with the revolution.

1965   His first marriage having ended in divorce, he marries Patricia Llosa, his first cousin. They have a daughter and two sons.

1966   His second novel, *La casa verde (The Green House),* appears, and firmly establishes his reputation as one of the leading figures in Hispanic American fiction. The novel wins the prestigious Rómulo Gallegos Prize.

1969   Publication of the two-volume novel *Conversación en La Catedral (Conversation in The Cathedral).*

1971   Publishes the first of several works of literary criticism, a revision of his Ph.D. dissertation, *García Márquez: Historia de un deicidio (García Márquez: Story of a Deicide).*

1973   Publishes *Pantaleón y las visitadoras (Captain Pantoja and the Special Service),* one of the few successful comic novels in Hispanic American fiction.

1975   Is appointed the Edward Laroque Tinker Visiting Professor at Columbia University.

1976   Named president of PEN International.

1977   *La tía Julia y el escribidor (Aunt Julia and the Script-writer)* is published, a novel based on his courtship of Julia Urquidi and his work as a writer for a radio station in Lima.

1977–78   Appointed to the Simon Bolivar chair in Latin American Studies at Cambridge University.

1981   Publication of the novel *La guerra del fin del mundo (The War of the End of the World)*.

1981   Publishes his first play, *La señorita de Tacna (The Spinster from Tacna)*.

1984   Publication of the novel *Historia de Mayta (The Real Life of Alejandro Mayta)*.

1986   Publishes *Quién mató a Palomino Molero? (Who Killed Palomino Molero?)*, a successful attempt at serious detective or suspense fiction.

1988   Publication of the novel *El hablador (The Story-teller)*.

1988   Is appointed the Jeannette K. Watson Distinguished Visiting Professor in the Humanities at Syracuse University.

1990   In a runoff presidential election in June, loses to Alberto Fujimori.

A WRITER'S REALITY

❖ 1 ❖

An Invitation to Borges's Fiction

As a student I had a passion for Jean Paul Sartre and I firmly believed in his thesis that the writer's commitment was to his own times and to the society in which he lived, that words were actions, and that through writing a man might influence history. Today such ideas seem naïve and may even invite a yawn. We live in an age of smug skepticism about the power of literature as well as about history. But in the 1950s the notion that the world could be changed for the better and that literature should contribute to this effort struck many of us as both persuasive and exciting. By then Borges's[1] influence was beginning to be felt beyond the small circle of the magazine *Sur*[2] and his Argen-

I would like to thank Professor David Robinson for his editorial assistance with this essay and several others.

1. Jorge Luis Borges (1899–1986). Borges was an excellent avant-garde poet in the 1920s and 1930s. But his worldwide reputation rests on his short stories, which he began publishing only in the mid-1930s. Among the most important volumes of stories are *The Universal History of Infamy* (1935), *Garden of the Forking Paths* (1941), *Fictions* (1935–1944), *The Aleph and Other Stories* (1949), and *Dr. Brodie's Report* (1970).

2. *Sur.* Influential liberal Argentine literary magazine of universal scope founded in 1931 by Victoria Ocampo and directed by her until her death in 1979. Borges was a member of the first editorial board of *Sur.* Distinguished Latin American literary figures — Borges, Eduardo Mallea, Alfonso Reyes, Vicente Huidobro, Gabriela Mistral and Octavio Paz — all contributed to *Sur,* as

1

tine admirers. In a number of Latin American cities, among the literary set, ardent followers fought over the scarcer editions of his books as if they were treasures and learned by heart those visionary random lists or catalogs that dot Borges's pages, the particularly beautiful one from "El Aleph,"[3] for instance, and helped themselves not only to his labyrinths, tigers, mirrors, masks, and knives but also to his strikingly original use of adjectives and adverbs. In Lima, the first of these Borges enthusiasts I came across was a friend and contemporary of mine with whom I shared my books and my literary dreams. Borges was always an inexhaustible topic of discussion. In a clinically pure way he stood for everything Sartre had taught me to hate — the artist shrinking from the world around him to take refuge in a world of the intellect, erudition, and fantasy; the writer looking down on politics, history, and even reality and shamelessly displaying his skepticism and his wry disdain for whatever did not stem from books; the intellectual who not only allowed himself to treat ironically the dogmas and idealism of the Left but who took his own iconoclasm to the extreme of joining the conservative party and haughtily justifying this decision by claiming that gentlemen prefer lost causes.

In our discussions I tried to show with all the Sartrean malice I could command that an intellectual who wrote, spoke, and behaved the way Borges did, somehow shared responsibility for all the world's social ills, that his stories and poems were little more than *bibelot d'inanité sonore* (mere trinkets of high-sounding emptiness), and that history, with its terrible sense of justice, which progressives wield as it suits them, like the execu-

---

well as foreign authors in translation, such as Faulkner, Huxley, Saroyan, Steinbeck, Camus, Gide, Sartre, and Valéry.

3. "El Aleph." One of Borges' most famous stories, in which the protagonist, the pedant Carlos Argentino Daneri, on the nineteenth step in his cellar, comes upon the Aleph, a point in space that is supposed to hold all possible points.

tioner's ax or the sharper's marked card or the conjurer's sleight
of hand, would one day build him his just desserts. But once
the arguments were over, in the discrete solitude of my room or
the library, like the fanatical Puritan of Somerset Maugham's
Rain who gives in to the temptation of the flesh he renounces,
I found Borges's spell irresistible. And I would read his stories,
poems, and essays in utter amazement. Moreover, the adulter-
ous feeling I had that I was betraying my mentor, Sartre, only
increased my perverse pleasure.

I had been somewhat fickle in the literary passions of my
adolescence. Nowadays, when I reread many of the writers who
were once my models, I find they no longer hold me, Sartre included. But the secret, sinful passion I harbored for Borges's work
has never faded; and rereading him, which I have done from time
to time like someone performing a ritual, has always been a happy
experience. Only recently, in the preparation of this essay, I read
all his books again one after another and once more marveled
exactly as I had done the first time at the elegance and straight-
forwardness of his prose, the refinement of his stories, and the
perfection of his craftsmanship. I am quite aware of how ephem-
eral literary assessments may prove, but in Borges's case I do not
consider it rash to acclaim him as the most important thing to
happen to imaginative writing in the Spanish language in modern times and as one of the most memorable artists of our age.
I also believe that the debt we who write in Spanish owe to Borges is enormous. That includes even those of us, like myself, who
have never written a story of pure fantasy or ever felt any particular affinity for ghosts or doppelgängers, the infinite, or the
metaphysics of Schopenhauer.

A writer is not always conscious of the influences he has received. Because I write realistic novels and short stories, my work
differs greatly from Borges's. But, again, I have been reading
Borges ever since I discovered him and always with great admiration. This attention has left some kind of mark on what

I have written, although I cannot say in what specific areas it is present. Many writers in Latin America have been greatly influenced by Borges. His influence on the prose of García Márquez[4] is well assimilated. In Julio Cortázar[5] the Borges influence is even greater because Borges's presence is obvious not only in the style but also in the system of transformation of daily reality into pure fantasy. This mechanism of transformation of real reality into imaginary reality is Borgesian. Borges also greatly influenced the Mexican Juan José Arreola,[6] a very good fantasy writer.

For the Latin American writer, Borges heralded the end of a kind of inferiority complex that inhibited us all unwittingly from broaching certain subjects and that kept us imprisoned in a provincial outlook. Before Borges it seemed a piece of foolhardiness or self-delusion for one of us to pursue universal culture as a European or a North American might. A handful of Latin American modernist poets had previously done so, of course, but their attempts, even in the case of the most famous among them, Rubén Darío,[7] smacked of parody, or whimsicality, something akin to a superficial, slightly frivolous journey through a foreign land. Actually, the Latin American writer had

4. Gabriel García Márquez (1928–   ). The great Colombian writer, Nobel Laureate 1982, is the author of *One Hundred Years of Solitude* (1967), *Love in the Time of Cholera* (1988), and *El general en su laberinto* (The Labyrinth of the General) (1989).

5. Julio Cortázar (1914–1984). Great Argentine fiction writer and political essayist. Among his writings are *Bestiario* (1951), *End of the Game* (1956), *Stories of Cronopios and Famas* (1962), *All Fires the Fire and Other Stories* (1966), and his masterpiece, the novel *Hopscotch* (1963), the story of an angry and confused Argentine expatriate.

6. Juan José Arreola (b. 1918). Mexican short story writer who uses fantasy and magic realism to satirize contemporary society. His stories are collected in *Confabulario and Other Inventions* (1952).

7. Rubén Darío (1867–1916). The great Nicaraguan poet whose *Blue* (1888) and *Profane Prose* (1896) are central works in the modernist movement that revolutionized Latin American poetry.

forgotten what our classical writers, like the Inca Garcilaso[8] or Sor Juana Inés de la Cruz,[9] never held in doubt, the fact that by right of language and history he was part and parcel of Western culture, not a mere epigone or a colonial, but a legitimate part of that tradition ever since Spaniard and Portuguese, four and a half centuries earlier, had extended the frontiers of Western culture to the Southern Hemisphere.

With Borges this became true once more. At the same time it was proved that to participate in this culture took nothing away from the Latin American writer's sovereignty or his originality. Few European writers have assimilated the legacy of the West as completely and as thoroughly as did this Argentine poet and storyteller from the periphery. Who among Borges's contemporaries handled with equal ease Scandinavian myths, Anglo-Saxon poetry, German philosophy, Spain's Golden Age literature, the English poets, Dante, Homer, and the myths and legends of the Far and Middle East that Europe translated and gave to the world? But this did not make a European of Borges. I remember the surprise of my students at Queen Mary College in the University of London during the 1960s. We were reading *Ficciones* and "El Aleph" when I told them there were Latin Americans who accused Borges of being Europeanized, of being little more than an English writer. They could not see why. To them, this writer in whose stories so many different countries, ages, themes, and cultural references are intertwined, seemed as exotic as the cha-

8. El Inca Garcilaso de la Vega (1539–1616). Born of a Spanish father and an Inca princess, he was the first mestizo writer in Latin America. Author of *Royal Commentaries of the Incas* (1609) and *General History of Peru* (1617).

9. Sor Juana Inés de la Cruz (1651–1695). The greatest Latin American poet of the colonial period, frequently called "The Tenth Mexican Muse." Her poetry is one of the finest examples of the baroque in Latin America. She is also the author of many dramatic works and prose writings that reveal an independence of thought rarely exhibited in literature by a woman of the seventeenth century in Mexico.

cha-cha, which was all the rage at that time. They were not wrong. Borges was not a writer in prison behind the heavy bars of national tradition, as European writers often are. And this freedom facilitated his journeys through cultural space, in which, thanks to the many languages he knew, he moved with consummate ease. This cosmopolitanism, this eagerness to be a master of so far-ranging a cultural sphere, this construction of a past upon a foundation both national and foreign was a way of being profoundly Argentine, which is to say Latin American.

But in Borges's case, his intense involvement with European literature was also a way of shaping his own personal geography, a way of being Borges. Through his broad interests and his private demons, he was weaving a fabric of great originality made up of strange combinations in which the prose of Stevenson and the Arabian Nights translated by Englishmen and Frenchmen rubbed shoulders with gauchos out of *Martín Fierro*[10] and characters from Islandic sagas, and in which two old-time hoodlums from a Buenos Aires more imagined than remembered fight with knives in a quarrel that seems the extension of a medieval dispute that results in a death by fire of two Christian theologians. Against the unique Borgesian backdrop, the most heterogeneous creatures and events parade, just as they do in the "Aleph," in Carlos Argentino Daneri's cellar. But in contrast with what takes place in that tiny pacific screen that can reveal the elements of the universe only at random, in Borges's work every element and every being is brought together, filtered through a single point of view, and given the verbal expression that lends it individual character.

Here is another area in which the Latin American writer owes much to the example of Borges. Not only did he prove to us that an Argentine could speak with authority on Shakespeare and

10. *Martín Fierro.* Classic Argentine epic poem (1872) of the persecuted gaucho, by José Hernández (1834–1886).

create convincing stories with characters who came from Aberdeen but he also revolutionized the tradition of his literary language. Note that I said *example* and not *influence*. Borges's prose, because of his quiet originality, has wreaked havoc among countless admirers, in whose work the use of certain images or verbs or adjectives established by him turns into mere parody. This is the most readily detectable influence, for Borges was one of the writers who managed completely to put his own personal stamp on the Spanish language.

Word music was his favorite, and it is as distinctive in him as it is in the most illustrious of our classics, namely Quevedo,[11] whom Borges admired, and Góngora,[12] whom he did not. Borges's prose is so recognizable to the ear that often in someone else's work a single sentence, or even a simple verb, *conjeturar* (to conjecture), for example, or *fatigar* (to exhaust; to vex), used transitively, becomes a dead giveaway of Borges's influence. Borges made a profound impression on Spanish literary prose as before him Rubén Darío had on poetry. The difference between them is that Darío imported and introduced from France a number of mannerisms and themes that he adapted to his own work and to his own idiosyncratic style. In some way all this expressed the feelings and at times the snobbery of a whole period and a certain social milieu, which is why his devices could be used by so many without his followers losing their individual voices.

The Borges revolution was personal. It represented him alone and only in a vague, roundabout way was it connected to the

11. Francisco de Quevedo (1580–1645). One of the great writers of the Golden Age in Spanish literature. Author of *The Life of a Sharper* (1626), a picaresque novel, and *Visions* (1627), grotesque pictures of hell and Judgment Day. Quevedo is one of the most acerb satirists in Spanish literature.

12. Luis de Góngora (1561–1627). Spanish poet of great renown, author of beautiful lyrical and narrative poems and also of obscure verses, such as *Solitudes* (1613), written in artificial and contrived language.

setting in which he was formed and which in turn he helped cru-
cially to form — that of the magazine *Sur,* which is why in anyone else's hands Borges's style comes across as a caricature. But
this clearly does not diminish his importance or lessen in the
slightest the enormous pleasure his prose gives. It can be savored
word by word like a delicacy. The revolutionary thing about
Borges's prose is that it contains almost as many ideas as words,
for his precision and concision are absolutes. While this skill
is not uncommon in English or French literature, in Hispanic
literature it has few precedents. Marta Pizarro, a character in
Borges's story "The Duel," reads Lugones[13] and Ortega y Gasset[14]
and this confirms her suspicion that the language to which she
had been born was less fit for expressing the mind or the passions than for verbal showing off. Joking aside, if we omit what
she says about the passions, there is some truth to her remark.

Like Italian or Portuguese or Catalan, Spanish is a wordy
language, bountiful and flamboyant, with a formidable emotional range. But for these same reasons, it is conceptually in-
exact. The work of our greatest prose writers, beginning with
Cervantes, is like a splendid display of fireworks in which every
idea marches past, preceded and surrounded by a sumptuous
court of servants, suitors, and pages, whose function is purely
decorative. In our prose, color, temperature, and music are as
important as ideas and, in some cases — Lezama Lima[15] or Valle

13. Leopoldo Lugones (1874–1938). Most important Argentine poet of
the modernist movement. Extremely influential in literary and intellectual circles
throughout Latin America. Among his volumes of poetry are *The Golden Mountains* (1897), *The Twilights of the Garden* (1905), and *Secular Odes* (1910).

14. José Ortega y Gasset (1883–1955), Spain's preeminent philosopher
and essayist, author of *The Spectator* (1916–1925), *Invertebrate Spain* (1923),
The Dehumanization of Art (1925) and *The Revolt of the Masses* (1930).

15. José Lezama Lima (1910–1976). Cuban poet and novelist, editor of
the literary magazine *Orígenes* (1945–1950). His most important novel is a complex, baroque work titled *Paradiso* (1966).

Inclán,[16] for example—more so. There is nothing objectionable about these typically Spanish rhetorical excesses. They express the profound nature of a people, a way of being in which the emotional and the concrete prevail over the intellectual and the abstract. This is why Valle Inclán, Alfonso Reyes,[17] Alejo Carpentier,[18] and Camilo José Cela,[19] to cite four magnificent prose writers, are so verbose in their writing. This does not make their prose either less skillful or more superficial than that of Valéry or T. S. Eliot. They are simply quite different, just as Latin Americans are different from the English and the French. To us, ideas are formulated and captured more effectively when fleshed out with emotion and sensation or in some way incorporated into concrete reality, into life—far more than they are in logical discourse. That perhaps is why we have such a rich literature and such a dearth of philosophers.

When Latin American thinkers set out to write philosophy, they usually write literature. This is true of the most illustrious thinker in the Spanish language in modern times, Ortega y Gasset, who is, above all, a literary figure. Philosophy comes to us through literature because it is difficult for a person of our culture to separate ideas from all the rest—flesh, color, sensation. Borges was a rare exception in considering ideas so important that all

16. José María del Valle Inclán (1870–1936). Spanish novelist of exquisite, ultrarefined aesthetic sensibility. Among his works are the four *Sonatas* (1902–1905), whose protagonist is the Marqués de Bradomín in four stages of his life.

17. Alfonso Reyes (1889–1959). Great Mexican literary critic, humanist, poet, and diplomat. His essays include *Vision of Anahuac* (1917), *Sympathies and Differences* (1921–1926), and *The Position of America* (1950).

18. Alejo Carpentier (1904–1980). One of Cuba's outstanding novelists, whose most important works are *The Kingdom of This World* (1949), *Lost Steps* (1953), *Manhunt* (1956), and *The Century of Lights* (1962). He also published a volume of short stories, *The War of Time* (1958).

19. Camilo José Cela (b. 1916). Spanish novelist; Nobel Prize in Literature, 1989. His early novels, *The Family of Pascual Duarte* (1942) and *The Hive* (1951) are among his best and most enduring.

the rest was eliminated, relegated to a second level. The genius of the Spanish writer has always flourished through excessive rhetoric, which expresses a fundamental element in our nature and in our culture. If you think of our great writers, all of them are great rhetoricians. Think of Pablo Neruda, for instance, a great poet. It is the exuberance, the excess. Creation is something that appears like a natural phenomenon, a kind of transpiration of nature more than an intellectual exercise.

Again, within this tradition, Borges's prose is an anomaly, for in opting for the strictest frugality he deeply disobeys the Spanish language's natural tendency toward excess. To say that with Borges, Spanish became intelligent may appear offensive to other writers of the language, but it is not. What I am trying to say in the wordiness I have just described is that in Borges there is always a logical, conceptual level to which all else is subservient. His is a world of clear, pure, and at the same time unusual ideas that, while never relegated to a lower plane, are expressed in words of great directness and restraint. "There is no more elaborate pleasure than that of thought and we surrendered ourselves to it," says the narrator of "The Immortal," in words that give us a perfect picture of Borges. This story is an allegory of his fictitious world; in it the intellectual always devours and destroys the mere physical. In forging a style of this kind, which so genuinely reflected his tastes and background, Borges made a radical innovation in the stylistic tradition of Spanish. By purifying it, by intellectualizing and coloring it in such a personal way, he showed that the language, about which, like his character Marta Pizarro, he was often so severe, was potentially much richer and more flexible than tradition seemed to indicate. Provided that a writer of Borges's caliber attempted it, Spanish was capable of becoming as lucid and logical as French and as straightforward and full of nuances as English. There is no other work in our language like Borges's to teach us that with regard to literary Spanish there is always more to be done and that nothing is final and permanent.

The most intellectual and abstract of our writers was at the same time a superb storyteller. One reads most of Borges's tales with hypnotic interest usually reserved for reading detective fiction, a genre he was to cultivate while injecting it with metaphysics. But his attitude toward the novel was one of scorn. Predictably, its realistic tendencies troubled him because, with the exception of Henry James and a few other illustrious practitioners, the novel is a genre that resists being bound to what is purely speculative and artistic and so is condemned to melt into the sum total of human experience, ideas and instincts, the individual and society, reality and fantasy. The novel's congenital imperfection and dependence on human clay Borges found intolerable. This is why in 1941 he wrote in the foreword to *The Garden of Forking Paths* that "The habit of writing long books, of extending to five hundred pages an idea that can be perfectly stated in a few months' time, is a laborious and exhausting extravagance." The remark takes for granted that every book is an intellectual discourse, the expounding of a thesis. If that were true, the details of any work of fiction would be little more than superfluous garments on a handful of concepts, which could be isolated and instructed like the pearl that nests in the shell. Can *Don Quixote, Moby Dick,* the *Charter House of Parma, The Devils,* be reduced to one or two ideas? Borges's statement is not useful as a definition of the novel, but it does reveal to us eloquently that the central concern of his fiction is conjecture, speculation, theory.

There is also an intellectual distance about reality in Cervantes that is very Borgesian. But in Cervantes, along with ideas there is always flesh, living experience reproduced, reinvented. Not in Borges. The literary world of Borges is much more abstract and intellectual than in Cervantes. That is why Borges despised the novel as a genre; because it is impossible to dissociate the novel from living experience, by which I mean human imperfection. In a novel you cannot be only perfect; you must also be imperfect. The imperfection that is essential in a novel was for Borges inartistic and, therefore, unacceptable. That is why he so often wrote against the novel and always depicted it as a minor literary genre.

Owing to its brevity and compression, the short story was the genre most suited to those subjects that prompted Borges to write. Thanks to his mastery of the craft, time, identity, dreams, games, the nature of reality, the double, and eternity—all lost their vagueness and obstruction and took on charm and drama. These preoccupations appear ready-made as stories, usually starting cleverly with quite realistic, precise details and footnotes, often concerned with local color so that at some point imperceptibly or even brusquely he can steer them toward the fantastic or make them vanish in philosophical or theological speculation. Never important or thoroughly original in these tales are the facts, but the theories that explain them and the interpretations that they give rise to always are. For Borges, as for his ghostly character in "Utopia of a Tired Man," facts are mere points of departure for invention and reasoning. Reality and fantasy are fused through the style and through the ease with which the narrator moves from one to the other, more often than not displaying devastatingly sardonic erudition and an underlying skepticism that keeps in check any undue indulgence.

I saw Borges very few times. The first time was in Paris, when I was a journalist. I went to interview him and was so impressed I could not speak. I remember one of the questions I asked him was "What do you think of politics?" He gave me an answer I have always remembered. He told me it was *una de las formas del tedio* (one of the forms of tedium). Initially, he was a very courteous, very shy man; but his personality changed when he became a celebrity. He adopted a public personality, very different from what he was before. He always repeated the same jokes. He made provocative remarks to *épater le bourgeois* (to shock the old fogeys).[20] But in spite of his remarks that sometimes

20. I think the reason Borges never received the Nobel Prize is because

seemed arrogant, he was one of the really modest writers I have met—modest about his achievements as a writer and about his genius. He did not believe that he was a genius. Until his fifties, he was an unknown man in his country. It was only when France and the rest of the world discovered him that he became a celebrity in Argentina and the rest of Latin America and that his life changed completely.

In a writer as sensitive as Borges, and in a man as courteous and frail as he was, especially because his growing blindness made him little more than an invalid, the amount of blood and violence to be found in his stories is astonishing. But it should not be. Writing is a compensatory activity, and literature abounds in cases like his. Borges's pages teem with knives, crimes, and scenes of torture, but the cruelty is kept at a distance by his fine sense of irony and by the cool rationalism of his prose, which never falls into sensationalism or the purely emotional. This lends a statuesque quality to the physical horror, giving it the nature of a work of art set in an unreal world.

Borges was always fascinated by the mythology and the stereotype of the hoodlum of the outer slums of Buenos Aires and the knife fighter of rural Argentina. These hard-bitten men, with their sheer physicality, animal innocence, and unbridled instincts, were his exact opposites. Yet, he peopled a number of his stories with them, bestowing on them a certain Borgesian dignity, that is to say an aesthetic and intellectual quality. It is obvious that these thugs, knife fighters, and cruel murderers of his invention are as literary and real as his characters of pure fantasy. The former may wear ponchos or speak in a way that apes the language of old-time hoodlums or gauchos from the interior. But none of

---

of his political statements, because he made rightest statements when it was unacceptable to be a rightest, to *"épater le bourgeois."* In fact, I do not think he was a rightest. He was a very courageous man; for instance, during the Peronist regime. He despised politics, but he opposed Peronism with great clarity and courage.

this makes them any more realistic than the heresiarchs, magicians, immortals, and scholars who inhabit his stories, either today or in the remote past from every corner of the globe. All had their origins, not in life, but in literature. All are first and foremost ideas magically made flesh thanks to the expert spinning of words by a great literary conjurer.

Each one of Borges's stories is an artistic jewel; and some, like "Tlon, Uqbar, Orbis Tertius," "The Circular Ruins," "The Theologians," and "El Aleph," are masterpieces of the genre. The unexpectedness and subtlety of his themes are matched by an unerring sense of structure. Obsessively economical, Borges never admits a word or scrap of information that is superfluous, although to tax the reader's ingenuity, details are sometimes left out. This economy of words might remind some of Hemingway, who was a sober writer, an austere writer. But the differences between him and Borges are enormous. Hemingway was not an intellectual. He seemed to despise intellectuals. His world is a world of facts, actions, living beings, things that are much more important than ideas. He was a realistic writer, something that Borges was not. The symbol of a setting for a Hemingway story is a boxing ring; for Borges, a library. On the other hand I think Nabokov was a writer quite close to Borges. He had the same rich literary culture, moved with great ease in different languages and traditions, and had a playful approach to literature—literature as an intellectual game, through which, of course, the real truths could appear. But apparently the game was for Nabokov just an exercise devoid of moral substance.

The exotic is an indispensable element in Borges's stories. Events take place far removed in space and time and, this distancing gives them an added allure. Or else they occur in the legendary outer slums of old-time Buenos Aires. In a remark about one of his characters, Borges says: "The fellow was a Turk; I made him into an Italian so that I could more easily fathom him." In fact, Borges usually did the opposite. The more removed in time or space his characters were from him or his readers, the better he could manipulate them, attributing to them those marvelous qualities with which they are endowed or making their often improbable experiences more convincing.

But this is not to say that Borges's exoticism and local color have a kinship with the exoticism and local color of regionalist writers like Ricardo Güiraldes and Ciro Alegría. In their work, the exoticism is spontaneous and stems from a narrowly provincial, localized vision of the countryside and its customs that the regionalist writer identifies with the world. In Borges the exoticism is a pretext. He uses it with the approval or the ignorance of the reader to slip rapidly, imperceptibly out of the real world and into that state of unreality which, in common with the hero of "The Secret Miracle," Borges believes is the prerequisite of art.

An inseparable complement to the exoticism in his stories is the erudition, the bits of specialized knowledge, usually literary, but also philological, historical, philosophical, or theological. This knowledge, which borders on but never oversteps the bounds of pedantry, is quite freely flaunted. But the point of it is not to show off Borges's wide acquaintance with different cultures. Rather, it is a key element in his creative strategy, the aim of which was to imbue his stories with a certain colorfulness, to endow them with an atmosphere all their own. In other words Borges's learning by his use of exotic settings and characters fulfills an exclusively literary function, which, in twisting the erudition around and making it sometimes decorative, sometimes symbolic, subordinates it to the task at hand. In this way Borges's theology, philosophy, linguistics, and so forth, lose their original character, take on the quality of fiction, and, becoming part and parcel of a literary fantasy, are turned into literature.

"I am rotten with literature," Borges once confessed in an interview. So was his fictional world. It is one of the most literary worlds any author ever created. In it, the worlds, characters, and myths forged down through the years by other writers flock in and out, over and over, and so vividly that they some-how encroach on the objective world that is the usual context of any literary work. The reference point in Borges's fiction is literature itself. "Little has happened to me in my lifetime, but I have read much," Borges wrote teasingly in his afterword to "Dream Tigers." "Or rather, little has happened more memorable than the philosophy of Schopenhauer or the word music of England." This should not be taken too literally, for any man's life, however uneventful, conceals more riches and mystery than the most profound poem or the most complex mental process. But the remark reveals a subtle truth about the nature of Borges's art, which, more than that of any other modern writer, comes of metabolizing world literature and putting an individual stamp on it.

His brief narratives are full of resonances and clues that stretch away to the four cardinal points of literary geography. It is to this no doubt that we owe the zeal of practitioners of heuristic literary criticism who are tireless in their attempts to track down and identify Borges's endless sources. Arduous work it is, too, make no mistake, and what is more it is pointless, for what lends greatness and originality to Borges's stories is not the materials he uses but what he turns those materials into. A small, imaginary world populated by tigers and highly educated readers, full of violence and strange sects, acts of cowardice and uncompromising heroism in which language and imagination replace objective reality and the intellectual task of reasoning out fantasies outshines every other form of human activity.

It is a world of fantasy, but only in the sense that it contains supernatural beings and abnormal events, not in the sense that it is an irresponsible world, a game divorced from history and even from mankind. There is much that is playful in Borges, and on the fundamental questions of life and death, human destiny, and the hereafter, he expresses more doubt than certainty. But his is not a world separated from life or from everyday experience or without roots in society. Borges's world is as grounded in the changing nature of existence, that common predicament of the human species, as any literary world that has lasted. How could it be otherwise? No work of fiction that turns its back on life or that is incapable of illuminating life has ever attained durability. What is singular about Borges is that in his world the existential, the historical, sex, psychology, feelings, instincts, and so forth, have been dissolved and reduced to an exclusively intellectual dimension; and life, that boiling, chaotic turmoil, reaches the reader sublimated and conceptualized, transformed into literary myth through the filter of Borges, a filter of such perfect logic that it sometimes appears not to distill life to its essence but to suppress it altogether.

Poetry, short story, and essay are all complementary in Borges's world; and often it is difficult to tell into which genre a particular text of his fits. Some of his poems tell stories, and many of his short stories — the very brief ones especially — have the compactness and delicate structure of prose poems. But it is mostly in the essay and short story that elements are switched so that the distinction between the two is blurred, and they fuse into a single entity. Something similar happens in Nabokov's novel *Pale Fire,* a work of fiction that has all the appearance of a critical edition of a poem. The critics hailed the book as a great achievement and, of course, it is. But the truth is that Borges had been after the same sort of tricks for years and with equal skill. Some of his more elaborate stories, like "The Approach to Al-Mu'tasim," "Pierre Menard, Author of *Don Quixote,*" and "An Examination of the Work of Herbert Quain," pretend to be book reviews or critical articles. In the majority of his stories, invention, the forging of a make-believe reality, follows a tortuous path, cloaking details in historical re-creation or in philosophical or theological inquiry. Because Borges always knows what he is saying, the intellectual groundwork for this sleight of hand is solid.

But exactly what is fictitious in his stories remains ambiguous. Lies masquerade as truths and vice versa. This ambiguity is typical of Borges's world. The opposite may be said of many of his essays, such as "History of Eternity," or the little pieces in *The Book of Imaginary Beings*. In them, among the scraps of basic knowledge upon which they rest, another element of fantasy and unreality of pure invention filters through like a magic substance and turns them into fiction.

No literary work, however rich and accomplished it may be, is without its darker side. In the case of Borges, his world sometimes suffers from a certain cultural ethnocentricity. The black, the Indian, the primitive often appear in his stories as inferiors, wallowing in a state of barbarism apparently unconnected either to the accidents of history or to society, but inherent in the race or status. They represent a lower humanity, shut off from what Borges considers the greatest of all human qualities, intellect and literary refinement. None of this is explicitly stated and doubtlessly it was not even conscious; rather, it shows through in the slant of a certain sentence or may be deduced from observation of a particular mode of behavior. For Borges, as for T. S. Eliot, Giovanni Papini,[21] and Pío Baroja,[22] civilization could only be Western, urban, and almost white. This civilization survives as it has come down to us, not directly, but through the filter of European translations of Chinese, Persian, Japanese, or Arabic original works. Those other cultures that form part of Latin America, the native Indian and the African, feature in Borges's world more as a contrast than as different varieties of mankind. Perhaps this is because they were a meager presence in the mi-

21. Giovanni Papini (1881–1956). Italian writer and critic, author of *The Life of Christ* (1923), *Memoirs of God* (1926), and *Life and Myself* (1930).
22. Pío Baroja (1879–1956). One of Spain's foremost and most prolific novelists of the Generation of '98. Rebellious and iconoclastic, he is the author of over sixty novels, among them *Paradox, King* (1906), *The Restlessness of Shanti Andía* (1911), and *The Tree of Knowledge* (1911).

lieu in which he lived most of his life. I also have had great difficulty writing about Indian characters in my own novels because I am a realistic writer in the sense that I write out of personal experiences. My personal experience of the Indian world is limited because, for one thing, I do not speak the Indian languages. I remember in writing *The Greenhouse,* I wanted to have an Indian character, a primitive man from a small tribe in the Amazon region, as the central figure in the novel. I tried hard to invent this character from within in order to show the reader his subjectivity, how he had assimilated some kind of experiences with the white world. But I could not do it. It was totally impossible for me to invent a persuasive description of a man who was so far away from me from a cultural point of view, a man who had, not a rational, but a magical relationship with the world. I felt I was making a caricature of this character and finally decided to describe him through intermediaries, through characters whom I was able to divine and to perceive.

Borges's ethnocentric limitation does not detract from his many other admirable qualities, but it is best not to sidestep it when giving a comprehensive appraisal of his work. Certainly, it is a limitation that offers further proof of his humanity because, as has been said over and over again, there is no such thing as absolute perfection in this world, not even in the world of a creative artist like Borges, who comes as close as anyone to achieving it.

◆ 2 ◆

Novels Disguised as History
The Chronicles of the Birth of Peru

The historian who mastered the subject of the discovery and conquest of Peru by the Spaniards better than anyone else had a tragic story. He died without having written the book for which he had prepared himself his whole life and whose theme he knew so well that he almost gave the impression of being omniscient. His name was Raúl Porras Barrenechea. He was a small, pot-bellied man with a large forehead and a pair of blue eyes that became impregnated with malice everytime he mocked someone. He was the most brilliant teacher I have ever had. Marcel Bataillon, another historian whom I had a chance to listen to at the Collège de France in a course he gave on a Peruvian chronicle, seemed to be able to match Porras Barrenechea's eloquence and evocative power as well as his academic integrity. But not even the learned and elegant Bataillon could captivate an audience with the enchantment of Porras Barrenechea. In the big old house of San Marcos, the first university founded by the Spaniards in the New World, a place which had already begun to fall into an irreparable process of decay when I passed through it in the 1950s, the lectures on historical sources attracted such a vast number of listeners that it was necessary to arrive well in advance so as not to be left outside the classroom listening together with dozens of students literally hanging from the doors and windows.

Whenever Porras Barrenechea spoke, history became anecdote, gesture, adventure, color, psychology. He depicted history as a series of mirrors which had the magnificence of a Renaissance painting and in which the determining factor of events was never the impersonal forces, the geographical imperative, the economic relations of divine providence, but a cast of certain outstanding individuals whose audacity, genius, charisma, or contagious insanity had imposed on each era and society a certain orientation and shape. As well as this concept of history, which the scientific historians had already named as romantic in an effort to discredit it, Porras Barrenechea demanded knowledge and documentary precision, which none of his colleagues and critics at San Marcos had at that time been able to equal. Those historians who dismissed Porras Barrenechea because he was interested in simple, narrated history instead of a social or economic interpretation had been less effective than he was in explaining to us that crucial event in the destiny of Europe and America—the destruction of the Inca Empire and the linking of its vast territories and peoples to the Western world. This was because for Porras Barrenechea, although history had to have a dramatic quality, architectonic beauty, suspense, richness, and a wide range of human types and excellence in the style of a great fiction, everything in it also had to be scrupulously true, proven time after time.

In order to be able to narrate the discovery and conquest of Peru in this way, Porras Barrenechea first had to evaluate very carefully all the witnesses and documents so as to establish the degree of credibility of each one of them. And in the numerous cases of deceitful testimonies, Porras Barrenechea had to find out the reasons that led the authors to conceal, misrepresent, or overclaim the facts, so that knowing the peculiar limitations, those sources had a double meaning—what they revealed and what they distorted. For forty years Porras Barrenechea dedicated all his powerful intellectual energy to this heroic hermeneutic. All the works he published while he was alive constitute the preliminary work for what should have been his magnum opus. When he was perfectly ready to embark upon it, pressing on with assurance through the labyrinthine jungle of chronicles, letters, testaments, rhymes, and ballads of the discovery and conquest that he had read, cleansed, confronted, and almost memorized, sudden death put an end to his encyclopedic information. As a result, all those interested in that era and in the men who lived in it have had to keep on reading the old but so far unsurpassed history of the conquest written by an American who never set foot in the country but who sketched it with extraordinary skill— William Prescott.

Dazzled by Porras Barrenechea's lectures, at one time I seriously considered the possibility of putting literature aside so as to dedicate myself to history. Porras Barrenechea had asked me to work with him as an assistant in an ambitious project on the general history of Peru under the auspices of the bookseller and publisher Juan Mejía Baca. It was Porras Barrenechea's task to write the volumes devoted to the conquest and emancipation. For four years I spent three hours a day, five days a week, in that dusty house on Colina Street where the books, the card indexes, and the notebooks had slowly invaded and devoured everything except Porras Barrenechea's bed and the dining table. My job was to read and take notes on the chronicles' various themes, but principally the myths and legends that preceded and followed the discovery and conquest of Peru. That experience has become an unforgettable memory for me. Whoever is familiar with the chronicles of the conquest and discovery of America will understand why. They represent for us Latin Americans what the novels of chivalry represent for Europe, the beginning of literary fiction as we understand it today.

Permit me here a long parenthesis. As you probably know,

the novel was forbidden in the Spanish colonies by the Inquisition. The Inquisitors considered this literary genre, the novel, to be as dangerous for the spiritual faith of the Indians as for the moral and political behavior of society, and, of course, they were absolutely right. We novelists must be grateful to the Spanish Inquisition for having discovered before any critic did the inevitable subversive nature of fiction. The prohibition included reading and publishing novels in the colonies. There was no way naturally to avoid a great number of novels being smuggled into our countries; and we know, for example, that the first copies of *Don Quixote* entered America hidden in barrels of wine. We can only dream with envy about what kind of experience it was in those times in Spanish America to read a novel—a sinful adventure in which in order to abandon yourself to an imaginary world you had to be prepared to face prison and humiliation.

Novels were not published in Spanish America until after the wars of independence. The first, *El Periquillo Sarniento* (The Itching Parrot), appeared in Mexico in 1816. Although for three centuries novels were abolished, the goal of the Inquisitors—a society free from the influence of fiction—was not achieved. They did not realize that the realm of fiction was larger and deeper than that of the novel. Nor could they imagine that the appetite for lies, that is, for escaping objective reality through illusions, was so powerful and so deeply rooted in the human spirit that, once the novel could not be used to satisfy it, all other disciplines and genres in which ideas could freely flow would be used as a substitute—history, religion, poetry, science, art, speeches, journalism, and the daily habits of the people. Thus by repressing and censuring the literary genre specifically invented to give the necessity of lying a place in the city, the Inquisitors achieved the exact opposite of their intentions.

We are still victims in Latin America of what we could call the revenge of the novel. We still have great difficulty in our countries in differentiating between fiction and reality. We are traditionally accustomed to mixing them in such a way that this is probably one of the reasons why we are so impractical and inept in political matters, for instance. But some good also came from this novelization of our whole life. Books like *One Hundred Years of Solitude,* Cortázar's short stories, and Roa Bastos's[1] novels would not have been possible otherwise. The tradition from which this kind of literature sprang, in which we are exposed to a world totally reconstructed and subverted by fantasy, started without doubt in those chronicles of the conquest and discovery that I read and annotated under the guidance of Porras Barrenechea. I now close the parenthesis and return to my subject.

History and literature, truth and falsehood, reality and fiction mingle in these texts in a way that is often inextricable. The thin demarcation line that separates one from the other frequently fades away so that both worlds are entwined in a completeness which the more ambiguous it is the more seductive it becomes because the likely and the unlikely in it seem to be part of the same substance. Right in the middle of the most cruel battle, the Virgin appears, who, taking the believer's side, charges against the unlucky pagans. The shipwrecked conquistador, Pedro Serrano, on a tiny island in the Caribbean, actually lives out the story of Robinson Crusoe that a novelist invented centuries later. The Amazons of Greek mythology became materialized by the banks of the river baptized with their name as they wounded Francisco de Orellana's [2] followers with their arrows, one arrow landing in Fray Gaspar de Carvajal's[3] buttocks, the man who meticulously narrated this event. Is that episode more fabulous

1. Augusto Roa Bastos (b. 1917). Paraguayan novelist. Author of *Son of Man* (1960), an almost mythical portrayal of the history of Paraguay, and *I the Supreme* (1974), a novel about a dictator.
2. Francisco de Orellana (1511–1544). Spanish explorer and discoverer of the Amazon River (1538).
3. Gaspar de Carvajal (1500–1584). Spanish chronicler. Arrived in Lima in 1538. Wrote *Discovery of the Amazon River* (1545).

than another, probably historically correct, in which the poor soldier, Manso de Leguízamo, loses in one night of dice playing the solid-gold wall of the Temple of the Sun in Cuzco that was given to him in the spoils of war? Or more fabulous perhaps than the unutterable outrages always committed with a smile by the rebel Francisco de Carvajal,[4] that octogenarian devil of the Andes who merrily began to sing "Oh mother, my poor little curly hairs the wind is taking them away one by one, one by one," as he was being taken to the gallows, where he was to be quartered, beheaded, and burned?

The chronicle, a hermaphrodite genre, is distilling fiction into life all the time as in Borges's tale "Tlon, Uqbar, Orbis Tertius." Does this mean that its testimony must be challenged from a historical point of view and accepted only as literature? Not at all. Its exaggerations and fantasies often reveal more about the reality of the era than its truths. Astonishing miracles from time to time enliven the tedious pages of the *Crónica moralizada,* the exemplary chronicle of Father Calancha,[5] sulphurous outrages come from the male and female demons, fastidiously catechized in the Indian villages by the extirpators of idolaters like Father Arriaga,[6] to justify the devastations of idols, amulets, ornaments, handicrafts, and tombs. This teaches more about the innocence, fanaticism, and stupidity of the time than the wisest of treatises.

As long as one knows how to read them, everything is contained in these pages written sometimes by men who hardly knew how to write and who were impelled by the unusual nature of

4. Francisco de Carvajal (1464–1548). Spanish conquistador who fought with Pizarro in the conquest of Peru.

5. Antonio de Calancha (1584–1654). Spanish chronicler. Author of the *Exemplary Chronicle of the San Agustín Order in Peru, 1638–1653* (1654), an extremely informative work on colonial Peru.

6. Pablo Joseph de Arriaga (1564–1622). Spanish Jesuit who taught rhetoric at the Royal Academy of San Marcos and became its rector in 1588. Wrote *The Extirpation of Idolatry in Peru* (1621).

contemporary events to try to communicate and register them for posterity, thanks to an intuition of the privilege they enjoyed, that of being the witnesses and actors of events that were changing the history of the world. Because they narrated these events under the passion of recently lived experience, they often related things that to us seem like naïve or cynical fantasies. For the people of the time, this was not so; they were phantoms that credulity, surprise, fear, and hatred had endowed with a solidity and vitality often more powerful than beings made of flesh and blood.

The conquest of the Tahuantinsuyo,[7] by a handful of Spaniards, is a fact of history that even now, after having digested and ruminated over all the explanations, we find hard to unravel. The first wave of conquistadores, Pizarro[8] and his companions, were fewer than two hundred, not counting the black slaves and the collaborating Indians. When the reinforcements started to arrive, this first wave had already dealt a mortal blow and taken over an empire that had ruled over at least twenty million people. This was not a primitive society made up of barbaric tribes like the ones the Spaniards had found in the Caribbean or in Darién, but a civilization that had reached a high level of social, military, agricultural, and handicraft development which in many ways Spain itself had not reached.

The most remarkable aspects of this civilization, however, were not the paths that crossed the four *suyos,* or regions, of the vast territory, the temples and fortresses, the irrigation systems, or the complex administrative organization, but something in which all the testimonies of these chronicles coincide. This civilization managed to eradicate hunger in that immense region. It was able to distribute all that was produced in such a way that all its subjects had enough to eat. Only a very small number of

7. Tahuantinsuyo. The name given to the Inca Empire in its totality.

8. Francisco Pizarro (1476–1541). The conqueror of Peru, unlike Cortes, was a rude, untutored soldier.

empires throughout the whole world have succeeded in achieving this feat. Are the conquistadores' firearms, horses, and armor enough to explain the immediate collapse of this Inca civilization at the first clash with the Spaniards? It is true the gun powder, bullets, and the charging of beasts that were unknown to them paralyzed the Indians with a religious terror and provoked in them the feeling that they were fighting, not against men, but against gods who were invulnerable to the arrows and slings with which they fought. Even so, the numerical difference was such that the Quechua ocean would have had to shake in order to drown the invader.

What prevented this from happening? What is the profound explanation for that defeat from which the Inca population never recovered? The answer may perhaps lie hidden in the moving account that appears in the chronicles of what happened in the Cajamarca Square the day Pizarro captured the Inca Atahualpa.[9] We must above all read the accounts of those who were there, those who lived through the event or had direct testimony of it like Pedro Pizarro. At the precise moment the emperor is captured, before the battle begins, his armies give up the fight as if manacled by a magic force. The slaughter is indescribable, but only from one of the two sides. The Spaniards discharged their harquebuses, thrusted their pikes and swords, and charged their horses against a bewildered mass, which, having witnessed the capture of their god and master, seemed unable to defend itself or even to run away. In the space of a few minutes, the army, which had defeated Prince Huáscar[10] and which dominated all the northern provinces of the empire, disintegrated like ice in warm water.

9. Inca Atahualpa (d. 1533). The last Inca, favorite son of Huayna Capac. Atahualpa was imprisoned by Pizarro on November 16, 1532, but released on ransom. He ordered the murder of his half brother Huáscar and was executed for the crime.

10. Prince Huáscar (d. 1533). His half brother Atahualpa and he shared the Inca Empire upon the father's death in 1525.

The vertical and totalitarian structure of the Tahuantinsuyo was without doubt more harmful to its survival than all the conquistadores' firearms and iron weapons. As soon as the Inca, that figure who was the vortex toward which all the wills converged searching for inspiration and vitality, the axis around which the entire society was organized and upon which depended the life and death of every person, from the richest to the poorest, was captured, no one knew how to act. And so they did the only thing they could do with heroism, we must admit, but without breaking the thousand and one taboos and precepts that regulated their existence. They let themselves get killed. And that was the fate of dozens and perhaps hundreds of Indians stultified by the confusion and the loss of leadership they suffered when the Inca emperor, the life force of their universe, was captured right before their eyes. Those Indians who let themselves be knifed or blown up into pieces that somber afternoon in Cajamarca Square lacked the ability to make their own decisions either with the sanction of authority or indeed against it and were incapable of taking individual initiative, of acting with a certain degree of independence according to the changing circumstances.

Those one hundred and eighty Spaniards who had placed the Indians in ambush and were now slaughtering them did possess this ability. It was this difference, more than the numerical one or the weapons, that created an immense inequality between those civilizations. The individual had no importance and virtually no existence in that pyramidal and theocratic society whose achievements had always been collective and anonymous—carrying the gigantic stones of the Macchu Picchu citadel or of the Ollantay fortress up the steepest of peaks, directing water to all the slopes of the cordillera hills by building terraces that even today enable irrigation to take place in the most desolate places, and making paths to unite regions separated by infernal geographies.

A state religion that took away the individual's free will and crowned the authority's decision with the aura of a divine mandate turned the Tahuantinsuyo into a beehive—laborious, efficient, stoic. But its immense power was in fact very fragile. It rested completely on the sovereign god's shoulders, the man whom the Indian had to serve and to whom he owed a total and selfless obedience. It was religion rather than force that preserved the people's metaphysical docility toward the Inca. The social and political function of his religion is an aspect of the Tahuantinsuyo that has not been studied enough. The creed and the rite as well as the prohibitions and the feasts, the values, and devices all served to strengthen carefully the emperor's absolute power and to propitiate the expansionist and colonizing designs of the Cuzco[11] sovereigns. It was an essentially political religion, which on the one hand turned the Indians into diligent servants and on the other was capable of receiving into its bosom as minor gods all the deities of the peoples that had been conquered, whose idols were moved to Cuzco and enthroned by the Inca himself. The Inca religion was less cruel than the Aztec one, for it performed human sacrifices with a certain degree of moderation, if this can be said, making use only of the necessary cruelty to ensure hypnosis and fear of the subjects toward the divine power incarnated in the temporary power of the Inca.

We cannot call into question the organizing genius of the Inca. The speed with which the empire in the short period of a century grew from its nucleus in Cuzco to become a civilization that embraced three quarters of South America is incredible. And this was the result not only of the Quechua's military efficiency but also of the Inca's ability to persuade the neighboring peoples and cultures to join the Tahuantinsuyo. Once this became part of the empire, the bureaucratic mechanism was immediately set in motion enrolling the new servants in that sys-

11. Cuzco. City founded in the eleventh century by Manco Capac. It was the capital of the Inca Empire at the time of the Spanish conquest in 1519.

tem that dissolves individual life into a series of tasks and gregarious duties carefully programmed and supervised by the gigantic network of administrators whom the Inca sent to the furthest borders. Either to prevent or to extinguish rebelliousness, there was a system called *mitimaes,* by which villages and people were removed en masse to faraway places where, feeling misplaced and lost, these exiles naturally assumed an attitude of passivity and absolute respect, which of course represented the Inca system's ideal citizen.

Such a civilization was capable of fighting against the natural elements and defeating them. It was capable of consuming rationally what it produced, heaping together reserves for future times of poverty or disaster. And it was also able to evolve slowly and with care in the field of knowledge, inventing only that which could support it and deterring all that which in some way or another could undermine its foundation—as, for example, writing, or any other form of expression likely to develop individual pride or a rebellious imagination.

It was not capable, however, of facing the unexpected, that absolute novelty presented by the balance of armored men on horseback who assaulted the Incas with weapons transgressing all the war-and-peace patterns known to them. When, after the initial confusion, attempts to resist started breaking out here and there, it was too late. The complicated machinery regulating the empire had entered a process of decomposition. Leaderless with the murder of Inca Huayna Capac's two sons, Huáscar and Atahualpa, the Inca system seems to fall into a monumental state of confusion and cosmic deviation, similar to the chaos that, according to the Cuzcan sages, the Amautas, had prevailed in the world before the Tahuantinsuyo was founded by the mythical Manco Capac and Mama Ocllo.

While on the one hand caravans of Indians loaded with gold and silver continued to offer treasures to the conquistadores to pay for the Inca's rescue, on the other hand a group of Quechua generals, attempting to organize the resistance, fired at the wrong target, for they were venting their fury on the Indian cultures that had begun to collaborate with the Spaniards because of all their grudges against their ancient masters.

Spain had already won the game, although the rebellious outbreaks, which were always localized and counterchecked by the servile obedience that great sectors of the Inca system transferred automatically from the Incas to the new masters, had multiplied in the following years up to Manco Inca's[12] insurrection. But not even this uprising, notwithstanding its importance, represented a real danger to the Spanish rule. Those who destroyed the Inca Empire and created that country which is called Peru, a country that four and a half centuries later has not yet managed to heal the bleeding wounds of its birth, were men whom we can hardly admire. They were, it is true, uncommonly courageous, but contrary to what the edifying stories teach us, most of them lacked any idealism or higher purpose. They possessed only greed, hunger, and in the best of cases a certain vocation for adventure. The cruelty in which the Spaniards took pride and which the chronicles depict to the point of making us shiver was inscribed in the ferocious customs of the times and was without doubt equivalent to that of the people they subdued and almost extinguished.

Three centuries later, the Inca population had been reduced from twenty million to only six. But these semiliterate, implacable, and greedy swordsmen who even before having completely conquered the Inca Empire were already savagely fighting among themselves or fighting the pacifiers sent against them by the faraway monarch to whom they had given a continent, represented

12. Manco Inca. Born in Cuzco, son of Huayna Capac and Mama Runta. Accompanied Pizarro when he entered the city. He was responsible for many raids on Spanish positions.

a culture in which, we will never know if for the benefit or disgrace of mankind, something new and exotic had germinated in the history of man. In this culture, although injustice and abuse often favored by religion had proliferated, by the alliance of multiple factors—among them chance—a social space of human activities had evolved that was neither legislated nor controlled by those in power. On the one hand this evolution would produce the most extraordinary economic, scientific, and technical development human civilization has ever known since the times of the cavemen with their clubs. On the other this new society would give way to the creation of the individual as the sovereign source of values by which society would be judged.

Those who, rightly so, are shocked by the abuses and crimes of the conquest, must bear in mind that the first men to condemn them and ask that they be brought to an end, were men, like Father Bartolomé de Las Casas, who came to America with the conquistadores and abandoned the ranks in order to collaborate with the vanquished, whose suffering they divulged with an indignation and virulence that still move us today.

Father Las Casas was the most active, although not the only one of those nonconformists who rebelled against the abuses inflicted upon the Indians. They fought against their fellow men and against the policies of their own country in the name of a moral principle that to them was higher than any principle of nation or state. This self-determination could not have been possible among the Inca or any of the other pre-Hispanic cultures. In these cultures, as in the other great civilizations of history foreign to the West, the individual could not morally question the social organism of which he was a part because he only existed as an integral atom of that organism and because for him the dictates of the state could not be separated from morality. The first culture to interrogate and question itself, the first to break up the masses into individual beings who with time gradually gained the right to think and act for themselves, was to become, thanks to that unknown exercise, freedom, the most powerful civilization in our world.

It is useless to ask oneself whether it was good that it happened in this manner, or whether it would have been better for humanity if the individual had never been born and the tradition of the antlike societies had continued forever. The pages of the chronicles of the conquest and discovery depict that crucial, bloody moment, full of phantasmagoria, when, disguised as a handful of invading treasure hunters, killing and destroying, the Judeo-Christian tradition, the Spanish language, Greece, Rome, and the Renaissance, the notion of individual sovereignty, and the chance of living in freedom all reached the shores of the Empire of the Sun. So it was that we as Peruvians were born. And of course the Bolivians, Chileans, Ecuadoreans, Colombians, and others.

Almost five centuries later, this notion of individual sovereignty is still an unfinished business. We have not yet, properly speaking, seen the light. We do not yet constitute real nations. Our contemporary reality is still impregnated with the violence and marvels that those first texts of our literature, those novels disguised as history or historical books corrupted by fiction, told us about.

At least one basic problem is the same. Two cultures, one Western and modern, the other aboriginal and archaic, hardly coexist, separated from one another because of the exploitation and discrimination that the former exercises over the latter. Our country, our countries, are in a deep sense more a fiction than a reality. In the eighteenth century, in France, the name of Peru rang with a golden echo. And an expression was then born: *Ce n'est pas le Pérou,* which is used when something is not as rich and extraordinary as its legendary name suggests. Well, *Le Pérou ce n'est pas le Pérou.* It never was, at least for the majority of its inhabitants, that fabulous country of legends and fictions, but rather an artificial gathering of men from different languages, customs, and traditions whose only common denominator was having been condemned by history to live together without knowing or loving each other.

Immense opportunities brought by the civilization that discovered and conquered America have been beneficial only to a minority, sometimes a very small one; whereas the great majority managed to have only the negative share of the conquest, that is contributing to their serfdom and sacrifice, to their misery and neglect, and to the prosperity and refinement of the westernized elites. One of our worst defects, our best fictions, is to believe that our miseries have been imposed on us from abroad, that others, for example, the conquistadores, have always been responsible for our problems. There are countries in Latin America, Mexico is the best example, in which the Spaniards are even now severely indicted for what they did to the Indians. Did they really do it? We did it; we are the conquistadores.

They were our parents and grandparents who came to our shores and gave us the names we have and the language we speak. They also gave us the habit of passing to the devil the responsibility for any evil we do. Instead of making amends for what they did, by improving and correcting our relations with our indigenous compatriots, mixing with them and amalgamating ourselves to form a new culture that would have been a kind of synthesis of the best of both, we, the westernized Latin Americans, have persevered in the worst habits of our forebears, behaving toward the Indians during the nineteenth and twentieth centuries as the Spaniards behaved toward the Aztecs and the Incas, and sometimes even worse. We must remember that in countries like Chile and Argentina, it was during the Republic (in the nineteenth century), not during the colony, that the native cultures were systematically exterminated.

It is a fact that in many of our countries, as in Peru, we share, in spite of the pious and hypocritical indigenous rhetoric

of our men of letters and politicians, the mentality of the conquistadores. Only in countries where the native population was
small or nonexistent, or where the aboriginals were practically
liquidated, can we talk of integrated societies. In the others, discrete, sometimes unconscious, but very effective apartheid pre-
vails. Important as integration is, the problem to achieving it lies
in the huge economic gap between the two communities. Indian
peasants live in such a primitive way that communication is practically impossible. It is only when they move to the cities that
they have the opportunity to mingle with the other Peru. The
price they must pay for integration is high—renunciation of their
culture, their language, their beliefs, their traditions and customs,
and the adoption of the culture of their ancient masters. After
one generation they become *mestizos*. They are no longer Indians.

Perhaps there is no realistic way to integrate our societies
other than by asking the Indians to pay that price. Perhaps the
ideal, that is, the preservation of the primitive cultures of America, is a utopia incompatible with this other and more urgent
goal—the establishment of societies in which social and economic
inequalities among citizens be reduced to human, reasonable
limits and where everybody can enjoy at least a decent and free
life. In any case, we have been unable to reach any of those
ideals and are still, as when we had just entered Western history,
trying to find out what we are and what our future will be.

If forced to choose between the preservation of Indian cultures and their complete assimilation, with great sadness I would
choose modernization of the Indian population because there
are priorities; and the first priority is, of course, to fight hunger
and misery. My novel *El hablador* is about a very small tribe
in the Amazon called the Machiguengas. Their culture is alive
in spite of the fact that it has been repressed and persecuted since
Inca times. It should be respected. The Machiguengas are still
resisting change; but their world is now so fragile that they cannot resist much longer. They have been reduced to practically

nothing. It is tragic to destroy what is still living, still a driving cultural possibility, even if it is archaic; but I am afraid we shall have to make a choice. For I know of no case in which it has been possible to have both things at the same time, except in those countries in which two different cultures have evolved more or less simultaneously. But where there is such an economic and social gap, modernization is possible only with the sacrifice of the Indian cultures.

One of the saddest aspects of the Latin American culture is that, in countries like Argentina, there were men of great intelligence, real idealists, who gave the moral and philosophical reasons to continue the destruction of Indian cultures that began with the conquistadores. The case of Domingo F. Sarmiento is particularly sad to me, for I admire him very much. He was a great writer and also a great idealist. He was totally convinced that the only way in which Argentina could become modern was through westernization; that is, through the elimination of everything that was non-Western. He considered the Indian tradition, which was still present in the countryside of Argentina, a major obstacle for the progress and modernization of the country. He gave the moral and intellectual arguments in favor of what proved to be the decimation of the native population. That tragic mistake still looms in the Argentine psyche. In Argentine literature there is an emptiness that Argentine writers have been trying to fill by importing everything. The Argentines are the most curious and cosmopolitan people in Latin America, but they are still trying to fill the void caused by the destruction of their past.

This is why it is useful for us Latin Americans to review the literature that gives testimony to the discovery and the conquest. In the chronicles we not only dream about the time in which our fantasy and our realities seem to be incestuously confused. In them there is an extraordinary mixture of reality and fantasy, of reality and fiction in a united work. It is a literature that is totalizing, in the sense that it is a literature that embraces not only objective reality but also subjective reality in a new synthesis. The difference, of course, is that the chronicles accomplished that synthesis out of ignorance and naïveté and that modern writers have accomplished it through sophistication. But a link can be established. There are chronicles that are especially imaginative and even fantastic in the deed they describe. For instance, the description of the first journey to the Amazon in the chronicle of Gaspar de Carvajal. It is exceptional, like a fantastic novel. And, of course, García Márquez has used themes from the chronicles in his fiction.

In the chronicles we also learn about the roots of our problems and challenges that are still there unanswered. And in these half-literary, half-historical pages we also perceive—formless, mysterious, fascinating—the promise of something new and formidable, something that if it ever turned into reality would enrich the world and improve civilization. Of this promise we have only had until now sporadic manifestations, in our literature and in our art, for example. But it is not only in our fiction that we must strive to achieve. We must not stop until our promise passes from our dreams and words into our daily lives and becomes objective reality. We must not permit our countries to disappear, as did my dear teacher, the historian Porras Barrenechea, without writing in real life the definite masterwork we have been preparing ourselves to accomplish since the three caravels stumbled onto our coast.

✧3✧

Discovering a Method for Writing
Sartre, Military School,
and *The Time of the Hero*

The process of writing is something in which a writer's whole personality plays a part. A writer writes not only with his ideas but also with his instincts, with his intuition. The dark side of a personality also plays a very important role in the process of writing a book. The rational factor is something of which the writer is not totally aware. And so when a writer gives testimony about his books, he does it in a particularly subjective way. He gives a clear picture of only what he wanted to do, which rarely coincides with what he actually did. That is why a reader is sometimes in a better position to judge what a writer has done than the writer himself.

My novel *La ciudad y los perros* was given the English title of *The Time of the Hero*. I must say I did not like it because *The Time of the Hero* does not give the same idea as the original title. But the title was chosen by my publisher. When I suggested "The City and the Dogs," he said that that title was not at all catchy; and so we gave the novel a more catchy title. But *The Time of the Hero* is not a real equivalent of the original title. I wrote this novel, which was my first (I had previously written a book of short stories), between 1958 and 1961. It took me three years to write this book, and it was an important experience because I discovered many things about literature and about myself, and I learned a method for writing that I have been practicing ever since in all my novels and other books. I learned two very important things about myself as a writer during the course of writing this book. First, personal experience is always the raw material for what I write. All my fiction—short stories, novels or plays—began as personal experiences. I wrote those works because something happened to me, because I met someone or read something that became an important experience for me. I am not always aware of the reasons why a particular experience remains in my memory with such vividness, nor why an experience gradually becomes a source of encouragement to invent or fantasize about. But all my fiction begins that way.

Among Latin American writers whom I admire and who also write directly from their personal experience is my fellow Peruvian José María Arguedas, who is not so well known abroad. He was an important writer, an interesting novelist and short-story writer and also an anthropologist. He had an intimate knowledge of Indian culture, something that very few writers have in Latin America; and he wrote interesting essays about Indian culture, about the Indian world. He was born in an Indian community and did not move to the white community until he was seventeen. All his books are a reconstruction of this Indian world that he knew intimately in his childhood. I read him with great admiration, and he probably had some influence on what I have written—particularly his first novel, *Los ríos profundos* (Deep Rivers), which was a great success in Peru, where it was first published. Although his experience is unique in Peruvian literature, there are other Latin American writers who had similar experiences in their own country: the Mexican writer Juan Rulfo, who also had direct experience in an Indian culture; and Roa Bastos, the Paraguayan writer, because in his books you can see that he had an intimate experience of the native world.

The personal experience that provided the raw material for

The Time of the Hero was the time I spent at a military boarding school, called Leoncio Prado, in 1950 and 1951, when I was fourteen and fifteen years old. I must tell you something about this school and about Peru at that time. Peru was and is a stratified society of not one country but many countries coexisting in a nation, with people belonging to these separate countries having little communication with each other. If, like me, you were a Peruvian born into a middle-class family and living in a middle-class district of Lima, you had a limited idea of what Peru was as a country, as a society. You might think that Peru was a country of white people, of westernized, Spanish-speaking people with a civilized and even prosperous way of life. You knew, of course, that Peru was also an Indian country, but you had no opportunity to see even one Indian if you were living in Lima, in Miraflores, a fashionable, middle-class district in the 1940s and early 1950s, because the Indians were practically all in the countryside, in the Andean region or in the outskirts of the city where a young boy of a middle-class family never went.

Thus my idea of Peru as a boy was distorted and restricted. I suppose this was more or less the experience of most Peruvians. Everybody lived secluded in a small world of his own with practically a total ignorance of what life was for other Peruvians. We were surrounded by a world of ignorance and prejudice that we took for granted was objective reality.

The divisions in Peru were many. First, racial: there was the Peru of white people, the Peru of Indian people, the Peru of the blacks, and the small minorities of Peruvians, the Asians and the people from the Amazon region. Second, there was the division between urban Peru and rural Peru, which are two separate worlds, completely different in customs and rituals, in the rhythm of life, and also in language because in the cities Spanish was spoken while in the countryside it was mostly Quechua or Amara, the native languages. Third, there were geographical and regional divisions, very strong today but even more so thirty-five years ago, among the coastal area, the Andean region, and the jungle of the Amazon. These three geographical worlds are like three different countries in Peru.

At that time there were very few institutions in which the whole country was represented. One of those rare institutions, really representative of all the complexity and the different social, cultural, and racial groups, was this military school, Leoncio Prado. It was a secondary school for only the last three years. It had been created in the late forties, and for several reasons there were young boys in the school from all social and economic classes. There were boys from the upper class who were sent there by their parents as a kind of reform school. They were difficult boys, rebels, difficult to control, who were sent there because their families considered that military discipline would be good for rebellious young people. There were many boys from the middle class who went to Leoncio Prado as preparation for a military career. They wanted to be naval officers, for instance, and thought that this institution would be a good training school for them. There were also many students from the lower class, even from the most humble and poorest families of the country. The first one hundred students who passed the entrance exam received a grant exempting them from tuition, and this policy opened the school to very poor boys from peasant families and workers' families and even boys from the slums, from the outskirts of Lima. So all the races and social classes and even regions of Peru were represented in the school, which was in a way a sort of microcosm of what Peru was.

The boys were between thirteen and sixteen years of age, and they all brought their own world to the school — their prejudices, their rituals, their particular vision of what Peru was. All these visions were competing one with the other. All the boys were subject to military discipline because the idea of the school was to provide both military instruction and academic education. When they finished school, the cadets received a reserve officer's diploma, which exempted them from military service. The school was put under the administration of one of the branches of the army, the infantry. We were organized like an army battalion and received very strict and serious military training as well as an academic education. I must say that this experience was important in my life. Now that I look back, I am grateful to the military school because I discovered what the real Peru was, of which I had no idea before I went to Leoncio Prado. But the experience was extremely hard for me. It was a kind of trauma. I had had a very protected childhood; my family spoiled me a great deal. And so when I went to the military school, I thought life was extremely kind; I had no idea that life could also be violence and brutality, that social, racial, and economic differences could mean real war among people. I had no idea that military discipline, the exaltation of military values, manhood, "machismo," and physical deeds could become something so violent and brutal.

I was shocked and terrified during the first weeks, maybe months, in that military school. On the other hand, in spite of the fact that I suffered considerably with the seclusion and all the violent rituals involved in military training, I enjoyed the school in one way. I learned how to read. I had always been fascinated with adventure and read novels of adventure voraciously. To learn how to read was extremely important in my life, particularly because I discovered this extraordinary possibility of experiencing an adventurous life through the fiction I read.

I suppose from an early age I dreamed of having an adventurous life, like that of one of the heroes of the novels of Salgari,[1] Jules Verne, or Alexandre Dumas—authors I read with enormous passion. This military boarding school was my first

1. Emilio Salgari (1863–1911). Italian writer whose novels were widely translated into Spanish. Among his works are *Carthage in Flames* (1908) and *The Accursed Man* (1916).

real adventure in life. Until then I had only fictitious, vicarious adventures through reading books, but the military school was a real adventure, brutal and violent but an adventure similar to those fictitious ones. The idea that I was becoming a sort of protagonist of an adventure similar to those fictitious adventures was something that helped me resist and tolerate the experience of being a cadet in a military school.

From my first weeks at the school, I knew that one day I would write a novel based on that experience. I immediately felt that that kind of experience was what I needed in order to write my own novel of adventure. And that is what I did. But it was impossible for me to do it when I was living that experience or immediately after. This fact was something I also learned from this first novel—that I needed personal experience to invent, to fantasize, to create fiction, but at the same time I needed some distance, some perspective on this experience in order to feel free enough to manipulate it and to transform it into fiction. If the experience is very close, I feel inhibited. I have never been able to write fiction about something that has happened to me recently. If the closeness of the real reality, of living reality, is to have a persuasive effect on my imagination, I need a distance, a distance in time and in space.

Thus it was with *The Time of the Hero*. I tried to write a novel based on that experience when I was in Lima at the university. I could not do it, even though I tried many times. But in 1958 I won a scholarship to Madrid to do my Ph.D. dissertation and started to write the novel immediately after arriving in that city. Six years separated me from Leoncio Prado, and there was, of course, the enormous physical distance between Madrid and Lima.

I said before that I discovered a method for writing, a method I have been practicing since then in all my novels and plays. The method is more or less the following. For me the most difficult part, the most difficult aspect is the beginning. It is especially difficult because I need to fight against my insecurity, which I doubt that I can ever overcome. The only way I can break this depressing situation is to write in an almost mechanical way, similar to what the surrealists call automatic writing. First, I always write a draft version of the novel in which I try to develop, not the story, not the plot, but the possibilities of the plot. I write without thinking much, trying to overcome all kinds of self-criticism, without stopping, without giving any consideration to the style or structure of the novel, only putting down on paper everything that can be used as raw material, very crude material for later development in the story.

As I begin writing a novel I have a general idea of what the story is going to be. I have some trajectories in mind, that is, the chronology of the action. One character starts here and finishes there, for example. I have this kind of information about the characters, a general outline of the story. But I never respect this outline, this plan. I need some general scheme, but I know that I will change it in many ways. What I enjoy in writing a novel is to discover the possibilities of a story. I know that my original idea for a story is going to be only the point of departure for something that will push me in an unexpected way. And that is what I enjoy, that is what I like when I write a book, to discover that something has been pushing me in a direction that I could not expect when I started. I consider that I have finished a book when I am so tired of rewriting it that I cannot stand the idea of continuing to work on it. Occasionally, I have been asked whether, after a number of years, I reread my work. I never do. Sometimes, when I am helping a translator, I go back to an episode. But I do not like to reread anything in its entirety because I always feel that I could have done much better.

The first version of a novel is always chaotic in the sense that the possibilities for the story are developed in a contradictory way. I write the same episodes two or three times from different points of view, from different perspectives. I sometimes develop contradictory trajectories of the plots, without trying to solve these contradictions or even changing the names of the characters or the places in which the episodes and anecdotes take place. And so it is a kind of magma that is very painful for me to write. But I know that when this magma is completed I will stop writing chaotically because all the possibilities are there, that my insecurity will vanish, that writing will become an enjoyable and exciting experience. All this I discovered in my first novel fighting very hard against myself. It was when I had this draft, this magma, that I started to feel what it means to create. That is why I say that what I really enjoy is not so much writing as editing a novel. Other writers, of course, approach their work differently. For example, Julio Cortázar did not rewrite a great deal. I was amazed when I learned that he wrote only one version of *Hopscotch*. The first version was the definitive version. When Cortázar sat down each morning to write, he did not know what was going to happen in the novel. He wrote the whole book in this spontaneous way, something that is for me unthinkable.

Writing a book can be a painful experience, but there is also pleasure. I would say that you have great moments of pleasure, great excitement, but they are a definite exception to the daily experience of writing. Creation really begins for me when I have a first version of the novel, when I have to choose, to select, to eliminate everything that is not worthwhile for the development of the story. When I discover that within this magma there are some logical and coherent trajectories and some forces, or drives, in the characters that must be followed and used, I begin to feel that I am in a process of literary creation, of inventing something. I always write a second version, in which I concentrate totally on the structure of the novel. At that time I am not concerned about language very much, about the use of words and phrases. I am entirely absorbed in the organization of the story, in the creation of the time structure in the novel. I did not know it at the time I wrote *The Time of the Hero*, but I later discovered that from a technical point of view there are two essential things to solve or create when writing a novel. The first is the invention of the narrator. I think the narrator is the most important character in a novel. In some cases this importance is obvious because the narrator is also a central figure, a central character in the novel. In other cases the narrator is not a character, not a visible figure, but an invisible person whose creation is even more complicated and difficult than the creation of one of the characters.

When I wrote *The Time of the Hero,* I was not aware of the role of the narrator, I was not conscious of it. Instinctively, I discovered that the creation of the narrator is extremely important because if you are not coherent in establishing the laws under which the narrator works, develops the action, approaches the action, or takes a distance from the action he is narrating, then the whole persuasive force of the novel will disappear. Therefore, coherence is what is important. You can give any kind of power to the narrator, but always within a coherent system. If the system is clear and coherent, the novel's power of persuasion will be achieved. If not, if there are incoherences and the narrator acts in an arbitrary way, this immediately translates into disbelief for the reader. The reader feels that something is wrong, that what he has been told is not really happening but has been imposed on him peremptorily. And so the narrator must be faithful to the laws that create the system of narration in a novel.

The second essential problem a novelist should solve is the organization of time. The narrator and time give fiction its sovereignty, its independence from the real world. A novel is never similar to the real world; a novel is always a separate world, a world that has something essentially different from real reality. It is a fictitious reality that is always in opposition to real reality. The difference between fictitious reality and real reality is the presence of this narrator, which in real reality does not exist, and of the time structure, which in fiction is never similar to that of real life. Chronology, the organization of time, and the way in which time flows in fiction are different from real time; and the organization of time is one of the aspects in which you can trace the originality of a fictitious world. The way in which each novelist, each fiction writer, organizes the time structure is what gives his literary work its originality and, again, its sovereignty. I discovered the importance of a coherent system for the narrator and for the time structure in *The Time of the Hero.*

One important influence in the writing of this novel, as we have seen, was my experience at the military school; another was the French thinker and writer Jean Paul Sartre. I read Sartre with great enthusiasm and admiration when I was at the university. At that time existentialism in philosophy was influential throughout the world and certainly at the university I attended in Peru. Sartre was particularly important in my discovery of modern literature, and I began to discover the importance of form in fiction while reading his novels and short stories. But most important were Sartre's ideas about literature, about what a writer should be and what literature should be. His ideas about committed literature were extremely important to me.

At that time I became very political, very much concerned about social problems, and I joined the Communist party in Peru. Because Socialist realism was the official aesthetic philosophy of the Communist party, I had a difficult relationship with my comrades in the party because I could not share this philosophy, this aesthetic doctrine of Socialist realism, which espoused literature as propaganda, as a vehicle to disseminate political ideas and the correct philosophy of the proletariat. Although I read much on Marxism during this period, I had these differences because of Sartre (who always had a love/hate relationship with Marxism), because Sartre's ideas about literature and the relationship between literature and history were so convincing to me that I could never accept the official doctrine of the party. I was never an orthodox Marxist; I was, for a short period of time, a very unorthodox Marxist. In *The Time of the Hero* you can feel something of the Marxist element, but I do not think it is evident in my later books.

I liked Sartre's idea that literature is not and cannot be gratuitous, that it is unacceptable for literature to be purely entertainment, that literature is serious because a writer, through his books, can be a voice in society, can change things in life. I knew by heart the presentation of *Le Temps Moderne,* a literary magazine Sartre published in France in the late forties, in which he said that words are acts that can produce social change, historical change, and that if a writer has this power he has the moral obligation to use it to fight for the victims of society, denouncing all the mystifications, all the wrongdoings of his time. I also liked Sartre's idea that literature is intimately linked with contemporary time, that it is morally unacceptable to use literature to escape from contemporary problems.

When I want to write about political matters, I write essays or articles or give lectures. I am convinced that creative literature is not a good vehicle for political statements. If you try to use literature as a vehicle for political propaganda, for the dissemination of political ideas, you fail as a writer. When I write literature, I concentrate on what is truly literature, something larger than politics. You can use politics for literature, but you cannot do the reverse. Literature should not be used to promote a political idea because the result will be damaging to literature. I have written novels in which politics plays an important role; for example, *Conversation in The Cathedral.* You can say it is a political novel because there are descriptions of a society subjected to a dictatorship and because political ideas and political actions are an important element of the work. But the novel was not written to disseminate political ideas. If what is compelling you to write is to make a political statement, you should not write a novel or use any other kind of fiction; for that it is much better to use a more rational genre, like the essay.

I believe the Sartrean ideas of social and moral responsibility in literature are profoundly reflected in what I tried to do in my first novel, which contains this kind of social concern. The military school, the life of the cadets, and their relationship with the military officers are a kind of pretext to describe the conflicts, the violent kinds of institutions a society like Peru has, as well as the economic and social injustices in that society. At the same time, Sartre's influence was present at other levels of the novel. In Sartre you not only had these ideas of the social thinker and social philosopher but you saw him as a writer, a writer of fiction and plays. In Sartre there was an unconscious fascination for the dark side of personality, for mischievous behavior, for torturous kinds of acts or inclinations or drives in human beings. It is interesting because Sartre is probably one of the most rational writers I have read, rational in the sense that he exercised strict control over his material. There is no feeling of spontaneity in Sartre's novels or plays. The impression you have as a reader of a Sartre book is that invention in his case was like a monstrous by-product of intelligence and reason, instead of the normally spontaneous creative drive that is at the core of most literature. In Sartre everything is rational, but in spite of that, there are always dark manifestations of irrationality in the characters of his novels or plays. His characters usually reflect the anguish of their lives. But through their behavior you can see the presence of something purely instinctive, something that cannot be really disciplined or controlled by reason.

I think that this attention to the darker aspects of human behavior also occurs in my first novel. The actions of some of the characters express the same kind of fascination for this torturous behavior, for this evil manifestation of personality. These characterizations probably come from my readings of Sartre's novels.

Another writer who also had an influence on the writing of *The Time of the Hero* was André Malraux, another French writer. His novels are not widely read anymore, which is a pity because he was a great novelist. I read his novels with great enthusiasm. And probably for all the many episodes in *The Time of the Hero* that describe collective action and the life of the cadets as a community, I had in mind the episodes in Malraux's novels in which he describes the scene collectively. I think he was a great novelist of the collective aspects of life. In *La Condition humaine* and *L'Espoir,* particularly, Malraux was especially successful in describing collectivity, the way in which great numbers of people act, in public demonstrations, in a war.

William Faulkner is another writer who had an influence on the writing of *The Time of the Hero.* He has had an enormous influence on Latin American literature, and I discovered his work when I was finishing my university studies. I remember that Faulkner was the first writer I read with a paper and pen, trying to decipher the structures, the formal creation in his novels. By reading Faulkner I learned that form could be a character in a novel and sometimes the most important character—that is, the organization of the perspective of the narration, the use of different narrators, the withholding of some information from the reader to create ambiguity. I was fascinated with this extraordinary mastering of the structure of a fictional work. I suppose this is also visible in my first novel. The organization of the story reflects some kind of fascination with these formal possibilities of the narrative form, the discovery of which I owe to Faulkner.

The story of *The Time of the Hero* is told at different levels. There are some characters who are presented to the reader only from an external point of view. The reader sees and watches the characters move and say things but does not know what has happened in the characters' inner selves. The reader is not aware of the motivation for their actions. Teresa, an important character in the novel, is an example of the external point of view. Not until the end of the novel does the reader discover that she is just one character. Until then she appears to be three different characters because she is depicted through the eyes of three different cadets who have known her at different moments and independently one of the other. And so they have a different image, a different idea of this girl; and only at the end do we realize that Teresa, who first is Esclavo's girl friend and then Alberto's, is the same little girl friend Jaguar had in his childhood and whom he later married.

On the other hand some characters are presented only from an internal point of view; and so while the reader knows what is behind their actions, behind their external conduct, this external conduct is itself closed to him. Then there are some characters, particularly the intellectual ones of the novel (there is a cadet who is interested in literature and another cadet who writes pornographic short stories), who are presented in both ways, simultaneously described from an external and an internal point of view. These different levels are not gratuitous; there was a reason for using a different perspective for each character.

For instance, the most contradictory personality in the book is a tough boy nicknamed by his fellow students "Jaguar." He has the public personality of a tough guy. He is the leader of a gang of four called "The Circle" and always acts as a tough and even brutal person in order to be respected. In a way, he incarnates the *machismo* philosophy that the officers and the school try to impose on the students. At the same time, he has a completely different secret personality, which he tries to hide because it would be a symptom of weakness—to reveal, for instance, sensitivity or emotions. So he presents himself only from an external point of view, only as he wants to be seen by the others. At the end of the novel, the reader will discover this other aspect of his personality and this one-sided character will become a more ambiguous and complex human being.

Another character, the most primitive in the novel, a cadet nicknamed "Boa," is a pervert who practices bestiality with a dog in school. He is described only from an internal point of view in a kind of stream-of-consciousness narration. This level represents the most instinctive aspect of life in the school. My experience at Leoncio Prado was that the whole philosophical and moral system that created the school's atmosphere had the capacity to give this instinctive aspect of personality an essential role in life. What I wanted to do through this character Boa was to show how the behavior of these boys could be seen as representing a distortion of this military philosophy. I wanted to show this only as a personal and intimate mechanism.

There are many sets of oppositions in *The Time of the Hero*. One is the world of the students and the world of the officers — childhood and adulthood. These two worlds are extremely different, even if they share the same philosophy, the same moral values, and the same social values. The officers do not know what real life is for the cadets, and vice versa. The cadets reproduce the lives of the officers in their own daily lives, in their secret lives. They reproduce the rituals, the way in which the officers treat each other; they reproduce not only the language but also the customs and the prejudices. But this is not a literal reproduction. When the cadets try to imitate the officers' behavior, those rituals become distorted, transformed into something different, into a kind of caricature. This opposition is carefully developed in *The Time of the Hero*. I suppose this was the most Sartrean aspect of the book. It was a critical attempt to show how the philosophy of this military world could destroy or orient the personality of boys in such a distorted way; how the idea of courage, for instance, perceived by a boy of thirteen or fourteen, could become a very brutal way of approaching human relationships and feelings. This distortion by the students of what the adults of the novel are represents the most Sartrean element of the work.

At the same time the different personalities the students have are very important in the novel. They are different when they are among themselves from what they are when among adults. They are different when they are with the officers and when they are with their families. And they are different when they are in school and when they are outside. It was as if the school created in them an aptitude for changing personality as a means of defending themselves against risks. That is why I used a phrase from one of Sartre's plays as an epigraph for the novel. "One acts the hero because one is a coward and a saint because one is evil; one acts the murderer because one longs to kill his fellowbeing. One acts because one is a born liar."[2]

What I wanted to express in this transformation of personalities in the novel was the necessity for the boys to become different as a measure of defense in life. That is something they learned in school. When I was finishing the last version of the novel, the third version, in the last episode I wanted the reader to know about two of the characters many years after they had finished the military academy. There is a conversation between this tough guy Jaguar and a friend who is a hoodlum, a man from the underworld (Jaguar had also been linked with the underworld as a boy). Jaguar meets this friend, Higueras, one day, and they have coffee together while reminiscing about the past. Jaguar tells his friend about his wife. He married a girl whom he had loved since childhood. When rewriting this episode for the third time, I suddenly had this idea: Instead of having Jaguar telling us how he ran into the girl he still loved, why not present this girl directly in the conversation between Higueras and Jaguar, without any kind of announcement to the reader, as in a film? When you are watching one episode in a film, and suddenly another episode remembered by the character appears, it creates no confusion for the moviegoer. Why not do the same thing in the novel and mix the conversation between Jaguar and Higueras with another conversation, another episode that took place years ago, something that is being recalled by one of the characters?

2. *Kean,* which Sartre "based on the play by Alexandre Dumas," *Kean ou Dèsordre et Génie.*

That is what I did. It took a great deal of work and head-aches to do it in a way that could be easily accepted by the reader. This technique became very important for the subsequent books I wrote. I discovered this way of mixing several episodes that took place in different times and different spaces into one sole epi-sode, an extraordinary possibility, a possibility I would explore and develop much more in my later books. That is the reason I mention this episode. I became so thrilled with the possibility of mixing times and spaces within one episode that my second novel, *The Green House,* is totally constructed around this idea of the *vasos comunicantes.*

❖ 4 ❖

On Being Nine and First Seeing the Sea
Writing *The Green House*

Writing a novel is a ceremony similar to a striptease. Like a girl who beneath the shameless stagelights frees herself of her clothes and shows one by one her secret charms, the novelist also denudes his intimate self in public in his novels. But, of course, there are differences. That which the novelist exhibits of himself is not his secret charms like the girl, but instead he reveals those demons that obsess him—his nostalgia, his guilt, sometimes his resentment. Another difference is that during a striptease, the girl is at first dressed and ultimately naked. In the case of the novel, the trajectory is reversed. At the beginning the novelist is naked and at the end clothed. The personal experiences that were the first stimulus to write the novel are so insidiously disguised during the process of creation that when the novel is finished no one, often not even the novelist himself, can easily hear that autobiographical heart that inevitably beats in all fiction. Writing a novel is then like an inverted striptease, and all novelists are discreet exhibitionists.

It occurred to me that it would be interesting for you, readers of novels, to attend one of these stripteases from which fiction is born. I would like to reconstruct in synthesis the process from which *The Green House,* the novel I wrote between 1962 and 1966, was born. The novel is situated in two very different places in my country. One is Piura, in the extreme north of the coast, a city besieged by great sand dunes. The other, very far from Piura, on the other side of the Andes, is a minuscule trading post in the Amazon region called Santa María de Nieva. These places represent two historical, social, and geographical worlds that are completely antithetical to and isolated from each other because communication between them is interminable and difficult. Piura represents the desert, the color yellow, Spanish Peru, and civilization. Santa María de Nieva represents the jungle, vegetal exuberance, the color green, Indian tribes that have yet to enter history, and institutions and customs that seem medieval. Within these two fixed settings the principal action of *The Green House* takes place. There is another area, the Marañón River, along which one segment of the story flows.

The origins of this novel occurred in 1945, when my family arrived in Piura for the first time. That year, which I spent in Piura as a nine-year-old boy, was decisive for me. The things I did, the people I knew, the streets and plazas and churches, the river and the dunes where my companions at the Salesian School and I went to play all remained etched with fire in my memory. I believe that no other period before or after has affected me so deeply as those months in Piura. For what reason? The problem intrigues me, and I have tried several times to understand it.

My mother says that the reason is that that year I saw the sea for the first time. Until then we had lived in Cochabamba, Bolivia, an inland city, and it seemed that the discovery of the Pacific Ocean excited me more than it did Balboa, to the point that for a long time I dreamed about becoming a sailor. Perhaps it was the discovery of my country, since 1945 was the first year I spent in Peru (my family had taken me to Bolivia a few months after I was born). In this period, between nine and ten years of age, I was a fervent nationalist. I believed that being Peruvian was preferable to being, shall we say, Ecuadorian or Chilean. I had not yet learned that one's native land is an accident in life.

But perhaps the main reason that my stay in Piura affected me so deeply was that in that year some of my friends, in an afternoon when we tried to swim in the almost dead waters of the Piura River, told me something that constituted an emotional earthquake for me: that babies did not come from Paris, that it was not true that white storks brought them to life from exotic regions. I suppose that until then I was convinced that I had arrived in this world on the soft, warm wings of that beautiful bird (which I had never seen), and that the stork had deposited me in the arms of my mother. The truth is that I was seriously offended when I discovered that things happened in a more humble way, and it took a long time for me to resign myself to the true origin of babies. Maybe that was the reason. Perhaps because I made the harsh discovery in Piura, all the events related to it in time and space entered my memory with equal tenacity.

Whatever the reason may have been, when I left Piura for Lima in the summer of 1946 I carried a constellation of images in my head. Some went away with time, others lived on pale and discolored; but two of them became more significant and vital every day. The first was the silhouette of a house built on the outskirts of Piura on the other bank of the river in the middle of the desert, a house that could be seen from the old bridge, solitary among the sand dunes. The house exercised a fascinating attraction for my companions and me. It was a rustic construction, a hut more than a house, and it had been painted entirely green. Everything about it was strange, its distance from the city, its unexpected color. Vegetation was rare then in Piura. The houses lacked gardens; there were few trees along the streets; and the walls, doors, and windows were usually white, yellow, or ocher, but almost never green.

Perhaps it was the solitude and humid exterior of the house that first aroused our curiosity. But more disquieting things further enlivened this curiosity. There was something evil and enigmatic about this dwelling, which we had baptised "the green house." We had been forbidden to approach it. According to the adults it was dangerous, even sinful to go near this place, and to enter it was unthinkable. They said it would be like entering hell itself. Adults became disturbed when we asked them about the green house. What happened inside? "Nothing, bad things, perverse things, don't ask silly questions. Be quiet. Go play soccer," they said. I suspected there was some connection between the green house and the destruction of the myth of Paris and the white storks, but I did not understand what, how, or why.

My friends and I did not dare approach the green house too closely because at the same time it attracted us, it terrified us. But we went to spy on it all the time. We had an excellent observation post on the old bridge. The most entertaining thing was to observe the green house at night because during the day this small building was calm and quiet, inoffensive. It seemed like a lizard sleeping on the sand. But at twilight the green house became a shining, living being, happy and full of noise. We could see the lights, hear the music, because at night there were singing and dancing in the green house. From the old bridge my companions and I could recognize the visitors to the green house, and that excited us even more. Hardly had the shadows fallen over Piura when the green house began to receive many visitors, and they were curiously all men. We spied on them and were shocked when we recognized our brothers, our uncles, our own fathers secretly crossing the old bridge. They became confused and alarmed if they saw us and became furious if they heard us shouting their names. They did not want people to know they frequented the green house, and to keep our mouths shut they bribed or punished us.

Another sport that my friends and I practiced consisted of recognizing one of the ladies who lived in the green house when she came to town to shop or to go to church or the movies. Another mystery was that only women lived in this strange house. I do not remember which one of us, perhaps I myself, one day began to call the fancy ladies *habitantas* and from then on we called them only that. We would recognize one of those elegant, proud ladies on the street, and we would run after her and surround her screaming, "*habitanta,* you live in the green house." And then the lady would lose her good manners, turn red, approach us, and, picking up rocks, terrify us with uncontrolled vulgarity. In school we had a professor of religion, Father García, an old, grumpy priest who became enraged when he found out we had spied on the green house or hung around the *habitantas.* Then he scolded and punished us. He was an avid stamp collector and his punishment always consisted in asking us for some stamps for his collection. Well, that formed one of the images that I took to Lima with me.

The other image was that of a peculiar area of the city called the Mangachería. Extremely poor people lived there, and most of their houses were flimsy mud-and-bamboo huts built on the sand because the Mangachería was also located in the desert, diametrically opposite the green house. This poverty-stricken neighborhood was the happiest and most colorful in Piura. On many of the huts were rustic flagpoles flying little red or white flags over the roofs; that is, these were taverns and pubs in which one could drink all varieties of *chicha* (a local beer), from the clear kind to the darkest, and enjoy the innumerable local dishes. All the musical groups, all the orchestras in Piura came from the Mangachería. The best guitarists, the best harpists, the best composers of waltzes and folksongs, and the best singers in the city were "Mangaches," from that neighborhood.

The neighborhood had a powerful, distant personality. The Mangaches were proud to have been born and to live in the area; they were Mangaches first, then Piurans, and last Peruvians. The rivalry between the Mangachería and the other neighborhood in Piura, the Gallinacera, had become legendary and given rise to terrible knife fights, to individual and collective battles. But at that time, the Gallinacera had dissolved into what we may

term somewhat ironically "civilization." And only the Mangachería still represented that old, colorful, factious, uncivilized
life of the city. A legend circulated in Piura about the Mangachería,
that the Mangaches had never permitted a police patrol to enter
the neighborhood at night. The Mangaches hated the police, and
the man in uniform who ventured into this neighborhood was
insulted, victimized by the taunts and rocks of the children, and
at times assaulted. The Mangaches detested the police, among
other reasons, because the Mangachería was also the breeding
ground for the most daring thieves and the cleverest criminals
in Piura.

That year, 1945, I read several novels by Alexandre Dumas.
They delighted me (and they still do), and I read them with that
pure burning passion with which one reads at the age of ten.
I remember very well, when the Court of Miracles appeared in
Dumas's novels, that hallucinatory neighborhood (according to
the image of it that the romantics gave us) of old Paris, the refuge of adventurers and criminals, how I immediately thought
of the Mangachería and visualized it. This identification persisted in my mind. I never hear the Court of Miracles mentioned
without seeing instantly the huts; the bars; the stray dogs; the
donkeys; and the noisy, rowdy Mangaches.

In Lima I entered the La Salle School, I grew up, and in the
years that followed many more things happened to me than I
shall narrate to you now. But seven years later I returned to Piura.
That was in 1952 and, like the first time, I lived in that city for
a year. I finished school there at the age of fifteen. The green
house was still there, in the same place, and the Mangachería
as well. Father García's stamp collection had grown, along with
his grumpiness. He was an old and irritable person, who, pant-
ing and shaking his fist, chased the children who were making
too much noise playing in the Merino Plaza.

By then I had admitted that the true origin of babies was
not so terrible, and that the subject even had a certain charm.

My classmates continued to be interested in the green house, and so did I. Adults still insisted that it was not proper to go to that place; but by that time we were no longer obedient, no longer feared hell, and physical and spiritual danger attracted us. We dared to approach and enter. Thus I got to know the green house from the inside. I confess that I suffered a bit of a disillusion. One found reality considerably beneath the rites and traffic with which fantasy had populated the green palace in the dunes. In fact, the palace became miserable and poverty-ridden; the mansion of our dreams was no more than an ordinary brothel. The ladies seemed less proud, shorter, less elegant, and more vulgar than seven years before.

But in spite of being so different from the image that we had formed of it, there was something enchanting and memorable about this brothel. It was an underdeveloped institution, lacking in comfort but certainly unique. It consisted of one enormous room full of doors that opened out onto the desert. There was an orchestra of three men; an almost-blind old man who played the harp, a very young singer who was also the guitarist, a giant weight lifter and professional boxer who played the drums and cymbals. In the corner of the room was the bar, a plank over two sawhorses, tended by an ageless woman with a bitter, puritanical face. Between the bar and the orchestra were the *habitantas,* walking from one side to the other or smoking as they sat waiting for their nocturnal visitors, who arrived with the dusk. Visitors and *habitantas* conversed and joked, danced and drank, and then the couples left to celebrate the rituals at the foot of the sand dunes, under the phosphorescent northern stars. This new image of that place coexisted with the old one when I left Piura in the early months of 1953.

I returned to Lima and enrolled in the university. My family was convinced that I should be a lawyer because I showed a strong sense of contradiction and detested mathematics. But in accord with my spirit of contradiction, I quickly exchanged law for the humanities. I wrote many poems and stories while I studied at the university, but without the idea of someday becoming a writer. It is quite difficult to think about being a writer if one is born in a country where hardly anyone reads — the poor because they do not know how or lack the means of doing it; and the rich because they do not care to. In that kind of society, to want to be a writer is not choosing a profession but an act of madness. In those years, then, I did not dare to harbor the ambition of one day being only a writer. One day I would say to myself, after all why not be a lawyer; the next day I would become a professor; and another day, perhaps the most sensible profession was journalism. I changed my decisions and my profession all the time and at the same time kept on writing in secret, like one who practices a shameful vocation.

Thus five years went by, and in 1957 I finished my studies. I began to work as a professor's assistant in a course on Peruvian literature at the University of San Marcos, and everything indicated that I would be a professor. The next year I received a scholarship to study for my doctorate in Madrid and was already packing my bags when a Mexican anthropologist, Professor Juan Comas, arrived in Lima. He came to Peru to investigate Amazon Indian tribes. The University of San Marcos and the Summer Institute of Linguistics had sponsored an expedition for him, and through my friendship with one of the organizers I had the good fortune to be a part of the small group that accompanied Professor Comas.

We were in the jungle a few weeks, traveling in a small hydroplane and by canoe, particularly through the region of the Upper Marañón, where the Aguaruna and Huambisa tribes[1] are found scattered over a large area. In this way I got to know that tiny locality, Santa María de Nieva, the other scene of *The Green House*. This trip through Amazonian Peru impressed me very

1. Members of the Jívaro group of Amazon Indian tribes.

much. I discovered one face of my country that I had completely ignored. I believe that until then the jungle was a world I sensed only through reading "Tarzan" and seeing certain movie serials. But by visiting the area I discovered that Peru is not only a twentieth-century country, as one can believe if one never leaves Lima or the coast, but also a country living in the Middle Ages and in the Stone Age. Thus I discovered that for those who live in this isolated region, life is behind the times and occasionally ferocious, that violence and injustice create the first law of existence, not in the complex, refined, "developed" manner of Lima, but in a more immediate, obvious way.

When I returned to Lima, I carried with me a small lizard embalmed by the Shapras, a bow and some arrows from the Shipibos,[2] and most important a wealth of memories from the trip. In the years that followed, three images stood out most vividly from the mass of things seen and heard. The first was the Mission of Santa María de Nieva. The town had grown up around this mission, founded in the forties, it seems, by Spanish missionaries who went to that inhospitable region in order to evangelize the Huambisas and the Aguarunas. We had a chance to know the missionaries at close range. We could see the difficult life they led in this place that was disconnected from the world during the rainy months, when the gullies that surround it become homicidal torrents. We could see the enormous sacrifice that remaining in Santa María demanded of them. But at the same time we could see how all this heroism, instead of reaching the goal that inspired it, achieved exactly the opposite. And we saw that the good nuns did not even remotely suspect that fact.

What happened? The nuns had built a school for the Aguarunas; they wanted to teach them to read and write, to speak Spanish, to wear clothes, and to worship the true God. The prob-

2. The Shapras and the Shipibos are also Amazon Indian tribes belonging to the Jívaro group.

lem had developed shortly after the school opened. The Aguaruna girls did not come to the mission, and their parents did not take the trouble to send them. The principal reason probably was that the Aguaruna families did not want their daughters "civilized" by the nuns. Why were they opposed to it? Because they suspected that once "civilized" the daughters would not wish to have anything to do with their tribes or families.

The problem was solved in an expeditious way. Periodically, a group of nuns went out accompanied by a military patrol to bring in girls from the settlements in the forest. The nuns entered the villages, picked out the girls of school age, took them to the Mission of Santa María de Nieva, while the patrol went along to neutralize any resistance. The girls stayed for two, three, or four years in the mission and were finally civilized. They learned the language of civilization, civilized habits, how to read, write, sew and embroider, and naturally the true religion. They learned to wear clothes and shoes, cut their hair, hate their former condition, and be ashamed of their old beliefs and customs.

But what happened when these girls were duly prepared for civilization? The problem for the nuns was enormous because in Santa María de Nieva nothing like civilized life existed; there barbarity reigned. What could be done with the girls, return them to their tribes, to their families? It would have been absurd and cruel to return them to a way of life which the nuns had systematically taught them to abhor, and which these girls probably now remembered with terror. It would be very difficult for them to adapt themselves to life as before—half-naked, worshiping snakes or trees, being one of the two or three slaves of a "cacique," a boss. Neither could these girls remain indefinitely with the nuns; they had to make room for new students.

How did the nuns resolve the second problem? They entrusted many of the girls to representatives of civilization who passed through Santa María de Nieva: officers from frontier outposts; merchants from Bagua, Contamana, or Iquitos; engineers or technicians who were engaged in petroleum prospecting in the region. Thus these girls from the jungle left for the cities, for Lima, where, foreseeably, they would live out their days as cooks or nursemaids, in the hovels of the distant slums, or in the green houses. Without wishing to or even realizing it, under tremendous hardship, the nuns of Santa María de Nieva were acting as the providers of domestics for middle class families and were populating the houses of the slums and brothels of civilization with new tenants.

The Mission of Santa María, the nuns, and the Aguaruna girls would remain a vivid reminder of that trip through the jungle. Another reminder was a man whom we met on the trip. In Urakusa, not far from Santa María de Nieva, we heard the story of Jum, the chief of a small Aguaruna settlement. He had come out to receive us; and we saw that his head was shaved, his forehead split, and his back and armpits scarred. The story began some weeks back when the corporal of the garrison at Borja, Roberto Delgado Campos, asked his superiors for permission to go to his native town, Bagua. The corporal set out on the trip from Borja accompanied by seven men. In Urakusa, when it became known that the group was approaching, the Aguarunas, fearing that there was a levy of soldiers, took refuge in the bush. The corporal and his men spent the night in the deserted community. They left the next day, their knapsacks filled with many provisions and valuable objects they had found in the town. When the Urakusas returned and saw that they had been robbed, they went in search of the thieves. They found them some days later as Delgado Campos and his men were sleeping in the forest. The corporal and three of his men were captured, beaten, and then liberated.

Some days later, an official expedition from Santa María de Nieva arrived in Urakusa to settle accounts for what had occurred. The lieutenant governor of Nieva commanded the expedition, which was comprised of eleven men. On seeing them arrive in his village, Jum came out to welcome the governor. The latter, when Jum was close enough, hit him with a lantern on the forehead. The Aguarunas began to run, but along with Jum, five men, two women, and several children were captured. The rest of the town disappeared into the forest. The prisoners were tied up in a hut in Urakusa, which the neighbors, excited and loquacious, showed us. There the prisoners were lashed and kicked by the soldiers who accompanied the governor. The two women were raped. One of them, the wife of a man named Tandím, was assaulted in front of her husband and children.

The next day, Jum was transported alone to Santa María de Nieva. They hung him naked from a tree in the plaza, and he was beaten senseless. They burned his armpits with hot eggs (I never understood how they did it). Humiliation followed torture: they shaved him. The lieutenant governor of Santa María de Nieva, the justice of the peace, the mayor, the lieutenant of the Battalion of Engineers, the school teacher, and a Jesuit missionary witnessed the punishment. After three days of torture, Jum was freed, and he returned to Urakusa. He spoke some Spanish and could tell us the story in detail.

The incident with Corporal Delgado Campos does not fully explain the violence that Urakusa and Jum had to endure. The basic reason for the brutality of the authorities of Santa María de Nieva was economic. Sometime before this episode, the Aguarunas had tried to organize a cooperative to escape the domination of the *patrones,* the men who controlled the rubber-and-hide business in the region. The tribes of the Upper Marañón lived there from the rubber that they sold to the *patrones,* or middlemen, who in turn sold it again to the industrial markets or to the Agricultural Bank. The *patrón* bought a kilogram of rubber that fluctuated between one and five *soles* and resold it in Contamana for a sum three or four times greater.

That was only one aspect of the system. The majority of the Aguarunas and Huambisas who provided the rubber did not read or write, and even fewer knew how to use the scales on which the merchandise was weighed. Thus on receiving the rubber, it was the *patrón* who determined its weight, always said to be less than it really was; the scales were accordingly fixed. Even worse, the exchange was not based on money but paid in kind. The *patrón* paid in machetes, guns, and clothes whose price he himself fixed. In this way the Aguaruna was always in debt to the middleman when he handed over his rubber. The gun, the machete, the food, and clothing he received were never paid for by the balls of rubber, so that once again he had to penetrate the jungle to extract more rubber, which some months later would increase his debt in a new transaction with the middleman.

This system had prevailed for dozens of years. It was a holdover from the rubber fever of the golden age of the jungle at the end of the last century and the beginning of the present one. That era was well past its prime. The *patrones* now were squalid, barefooted, semiliterate men of primitive customs. The rubber and skins of the Amazon were no longer a good business. In the Upper Marañón, man's exploitation of his fellow man reached the limits of bestial violence, but the beneficiaries of that horror obtained from it only a bare survival rather than riches or wellbeing. The poverty of the region and the anachronism of its society demanded that exploitation be extended to the most microscopic levels.

In the government's "education plan" for the jungle, a system had been devised at that time that consisted of sending the most intelligent, spirited men of the tribes to take a two or three months' course in Yarinacocha, where the headquarters of the Summer Institute of Linguistics was located, so that later they could return to their tribes and open schools. Jum had received this training at Yarinacocha. I do not know whether this short excursion into "civilization" made good teachers of the group of Aguarunas. But it opened the eyes of some to a concrete problem, that of finding out the true value of money and things, the abuse of which made them victims because of the underhand work of the *patrones*. They discovered that if instead of selling the balls of rubber and skins to the middleman they sold them directly in the cities, they would obtain much greater profits; and also that the objects they received from the *patrones* in exchange for the rubber would cost much less if they were bought in stores.

Thus was born the idea of forming an Aguaruna cooperative, and Jum had been one of the promoters of the idea. A meeting of mayors of ten or twelve settlements in which the Aguarunas are dispersed along the Upper Marañón took place in Chicais; and there Jum and the other teachers had convinced their people to stop trading with the *patrones,* and instead to collect the rubber and skins from each town in Chicais in order to make an expedition once a year to Iquitos to sell them directly to the industrialists. They constructed a large building to serve as a warehouse. We knew the building in Chicais, for there we had hung mosquito netting but had spent a sleepless night because of the horrible smell of rubber and the jaguar and alligator skins.

The Aguaruna cooperative project was the death sentence for the *patrones'* business. It was for that reason that the authorities of Santa María de Nieva—the *patrones* of the region—had punished Urakusa and Jum under the pretext of the Delgado Campos incident. They had admitted that fact to Jum while they tortured him; and when they permitted him to return to his village, they ordered the Aguarunas to forget about selling things themselves in the city. Jum's face and his story would form one of the most important memories of our trip through the jungle.

Another recollection I have of that trip is that of a man we never saw. I knew his history or rather his legend by hearsay. Everyone spoke of him; he was the center of rumors and gossip in all the towns and villages where we stopped in the Upper Marañón. His deeds became myths that in each place were retold with the additions and deletions of local fantasy. Everyone said that he was a devil, but they said it with open admiration.

Who was this man? What was his history? I will reconstruct as well as I can the swell of contradictory facts that we collected here and there. He had been seen many years ago going up the Marañón, and in the places where he stopped he announced his plan to go up the Santiago River to a territory where the Huambisas were thinly dispersed. No one knew where he came from or why he had chosen that densely overgrown territory to settle. He was a Japanese named Tushía.

During World War II the Japanese were harassed in Peru; and Tushía was fleeing from that harassment, according to some, or from crimes he had committed in Iquitos, according to others. People had tried to dissuade him from going on in that inhospitable and faraway region. In those days the Huambisas had hardly any contact with the civilized world, and tales of blood and ferocity were woven around these people, just as around all Peruvian and Ecuadorian tribes. "Don't go there, don't be crazy, the Huambisas are dangerous," the Christians of the towns through which he would pass told Tushía. "They will eat you, they will kill you," they said. The mysterious Japanese did not follow their advice but went up the Santiago River and settled on a small island in the densest part of the region very close to the Ecuadorian border and remained there until his death.

In a few years, this extraordinary person became a shady, enigmatic feudal lord. The Huambisas did not kill him, but it was a miracle that he did not kill all the Huambisas. Tushía organized a small personal army made of up outcast Aguarunas and Huambisas, men who for some reason had been expelled from their tribes, of soldiers who had deserted the border garrisons, and of other "Christian" adventurers like himself. Tushía and his men periodically assaulted the Aguaruna and Huambisa tribes during the times they knew that the rubber and skins were being collected to be handed over to the *patrones*. Then, through intermediaries, he sold his merchandise in the cities. He also sequestered girls. This particularly was the reason for his popularity in the region and the envious cult that formed around him. Tushía's harem became a myth; some said that it contained ten girls; others, twenty or more. Each man populated the harem with the number he would have liked for himself.

Some years later, during a second trip to the jungle, in a settlement called Nazareth, I heard the testimony of a man who had known Tushía and had seen him invading a tribe with his band. It was a baroque, sensuous ceremony more complicated and artistic than simple pillage. Once the village was occupied and the resistance of the natives conquered, Tushía dressed himself up as an Aguaruna. He painted his face and body with *achiote*[3] and *rupiña*[4] like the natives and presided over a great celebration in which he danced and drank *masato*[5] until he fell unconscious.

He had learned the Aguaruna and Huambisa languages perfectly; and he liked to dance, sing, and get drunk with those from whom he stole rubber and women. This story did not belong mainly to the past; it was happening at the same time that it was being told to us. It had been repeated for many years, with absolute impunity, almost before our very eyes. The embarrassed Mission of Santa María de Nieva, Jum's punishment, and the legend of Tushía form the three images that captured for me this trip through the jungle. I had conflicting emotions. Now I understand all of it better, but a few years ago it embarrassed me to admit it. On the one hand all that barbarity infuriated me; it made my country's backwardness, injustice, and lack of culture even more evident. On the other hand it all fascinated me; what formidable material to narrate!

From the beginning I thought about writing something about all this, and kept a notebook full of notes taken on the trip. I

3. The seeds of this tree are pounded into a red paste used as a dye.
4. A plant akin to the yucca from which a dye is made.
5. A fermented drink made from corn or from the yucca or manioc plant.

stayed a few weeks in Lima and then left for Europe. In Europe I first wrote a book of short stories, then my first novel, *The Time of the Hero.* After that, I decided to write another novel based on my recollections of Piura and the jungle. After I finished *The Time of the Hero,* I felt ill, disgusted with literature. Then I conceived the project, curiously therapeutic, of writing two novels simultaneously. I thought that writing two would be less distressing than writing one by itself because to go from one to the other would be refreshing, rejuvenating. A grave mistake. It worked out just the opposite. Instead of abating them, the headaches, problems, and anxieties doubled. I lived in Paris at that time and earned my living as a journalist and professor.

That was how in 1962, in a creaking but glorious (because Gérard Philipe[6] had lived downstairs) apartment on Rue de Tournon, those memories of Piura—the green house and the Mangachería—and the jungle—the Mission of Santa María de Nieva, Jum, and Tushía—returned to my mind. I had rarely thought of them in the intervening years, but now those images returned stronger and sharper than ever. As I mentioned, I had decided to write two novels: one, situated in Piura, based on my memories of that city, and the other in Santa María de Nieva, availing myself of what I remembered of the nuns, of Urakusa, and of Tushía. I began to work according to a rather rigid plan, one day on one novel, the next day on the other. I worked with these parallel stories for a few weeks or perhaps months. The work soon began to be painful; as the world of each novel was developing and taking shape, I had to make a greater effort to keep each one separate and independent in my mind.

In truth, I could not carry out my plan. Each day, each night I had to confront tremendous confusion. Absurdly, my principal effort consisted of keeping each character in its proper place.

6. Gérard Philipe (1922–1959). One of France's most popular and most versatile actors.

The Piurans invaded Santa María de Nieva, the inhabitants of the jungle fought to sneak into the green house. It became harder and harder to hold each character in his respective world. It was too tiring to keep on fighting to separate them. Then I decided not to do it any longer; I decided to combine those two worlds, to write a single novel that would embrace that whole mass of reminiscences. It took me another three years and much tribulation to bring order to such disordered material.

I had two distinct images of the green house. The first, that palace in the dunes that I had seen only from the outside and from faraway, and more with my imagination than with my eyes when I was a nine-year-old child. The second, the poor brothel where we went seven years later on Saturdays with good tips as fifth-year students at the San Miguel School. In the novel, these two images were converted into two green houses—two houses separated in time and space and constructed on different planes of reality. The first, the fabulous green house, became a remote, legendary brothel whose bloody history would be known only through the memories, fantasies, gossip, and lies of the people of the Mangachería. The second would be real and objective, somewhat like the other half, the pedestrian and immediate reverse of the mythical, uncertain institution, a reasonably priced brothel where the Mangaches went to chat, get drunk, and purchase love.

I remember quite well the faces and (although I am not completely certain) the names of the three members of the orchestra in the brothel: Anselmo, the old blind harpist; Alejandro, the young singer and guitar player; and Bolas, the muscular drum-and-cymbal player. I kept those faces and names in the novel, but to those elusive silhouettes I had to add biographies replete with anecdotes. Young Alejandro had a romantic name and romantic features; I invented for him a sentimental love story like those told in Peruvian waltzes. Bolas's impressive physical appearance suggested to me a classical stereotype: the giant with the tender, generous heart like Porthos in *The Three Musketeers* or Lotario in *Mandrake the Magician*. In Anselmo I revived a character dear to all enthusiasts of novels of chivalry and adventure films, especially Westerns: the stranger from afar who comes to a city and conquers it. I had always had a weakness for Mexican melodrama, and to humanize this lonely stranger a little, I added to Anselmo's story a decidedly truculent amorous episode. To do that, I used my recollection of a novel by Paul Bowles, *The Sheltering Sky*. At one point in this novel a man says (actually, or in his dreams) to a woman, "I want you to be blind, so I can terrify you, love you by surprise, play with you."

Ever since I read that novel, I have felt a perverse need to write a love story whose protagonist would be blind. To make Anselmo's passion even more sinister, I decided that Antonia, the girl with whom he falls in love, should be mute as well as blind. I remembered that in Piura matrimonial kidnappings were frequent, sometimes with the discreet consent of the respective families. The lover carried his beloved away to a ranch, the friends said goodbye to the couple on the highway, and a month later the wedding was formalized with due process of law. Anselmo would kidnap Antonia, carry her away to live in "the green house," where she would later die. All this, besides, had Faulknerian overtones because for me Faulkner was the paradigm of novelists. There are, of course, many reasons for a Latin American writer to be influenced by Faulkner. First is the literary importance of Faulkner's work; he is probably the most important novelist of our time, the most original, the most rich. He created a world as rich as the richest narrative worlds of the nineteenth century. But there are more specific reasons for which Faulkner has such appeal in Latin America. The world out of which he created his own world is quite similar to a Latin American world. In the Deep South, as in Latin America, two different cultures coexist, two different historical traditions, two different races — all forming a difficult coexistence full of prejudice and violence. There also exists the extraordinary importance of the past, which is always present in contemporary life. In Latin America, we have the same thing. The world of Faulkner is preindustrial, or, at least, resisting industrialization, modernization, urbanization — exactly like many Latin American societies. Out of all this, Faulkner created a personal world, with a richness of technique and form. It is understandable that to a Latin American who works with such similar sources, the techniques and formal inventions of Faulkner hold strong appeal.

It turned out to be quite difficult to narrate the love story of Antonia and Anselmo. The subject was so bizarre that it seemed incredible. I tried to narrate it from Anselmo's point of view, then from that of Antonia, and then from the indirect point of view of a group of Mangaches who evoked the episode at a table in a bar, but none of these forms seemed convincing. One day, I can no longer remember how, I found the right formula for putting that "terrible romance" into words. This was the idea. The story of Anselmo and Antonia would be narrated not as it really happened (that would never be known), but as the Mangaches supposed or wanted it to happen. In the novel, the existence of this sentimental adventure would have the same vacillating, subjective character as the first green house. It occurred to me then (only after throwing many rough drafts into the wastebasket did this form take shape) to introduce a narrative voice different from that of the impersonal narrator that would represent the conscience, or soul, of the Mangachería and that would literally put in order, by means of commands, the love story of Anselmo and Antoñita.

All of this had to be carefully ambiguous. The voice would at times be so close to Anselmo's own that it would seem to mix with his, to be his. But at the same time it would have a liquid quality; a certain atemporality; a suspicious, solemn tone that would denote in some way the mythical background of this story.

I worked with discipline and with an enthusiasm that never

diminished. I worked nights at Radio-Télévision Française, but I had the whole day to myself. I got up at twelve and immediately after showering sat down at the typewriter to write until seven or eight at night. I did not have the least difficulty in evoking Piura. I just had to close my eyes to see its narrow streets, its high sidewalks, its houses with wide grilled windows, and to hear the rhythmical and catchy local speech, similar to that of the Mexicans. I remembered the local sayings; and my room was full of *churres, piajenos, guás,*[7] and those unforgettable superlatives. It was all there in my memory, palpitating and unharmed.

To evoke Santa María de Nieva and the Amazon was, however, an exhausting effort: a few events, facts, certain situations, some faces, and a handful of anecdotes were all the raw material I had to work with to try to recover that immense world. My ignorance of that environment tormented me; I knew nothing of the trees, the animals, of mores and local customs. For an entire year I read whatever I could find in the Parisian bookstores and libraries on the subject of the Amazon. I can modestly say that I have read the worst, the most absurd literature in the world. Once a week I went to the Jardin des Plantes to see the trees and flowers of the Amazon, and one of the guards probably took me for a diligent botany student. Actually, these Amazonian texts immunized me against excessive description, and in the end I would only describe in my book a tree that I could not see in Paris, the lupuna, an enormous hump-backed tree that appears in jungle stories as the abode of evil spirits.

From time to time I also went to observe jungle animals in the zoo at the Bois de Vincennes; and every time I saw a puma or a vicuña, I remembered what another Peruvian writer who had also lived in Paris many years wrote. This writer, Ventura

---

7. *Churres:* grime, filth, anything greasy. *Piajenos:* donkeys. *Guás:* interjection expressing fear or surprise.

García Calderón, commented that when he would pass by the llama's cage, the animal's eyes would fill with tears of sadness upon recognizing a compatriot.

I changed the unclear legend I had heard of Tushía for a more sordid and concrete story, that of a pathetic adventurer obsessed with the idea of becoming rich, who during the course of his life commits horrifying atrocities to reach his goal but fails in all his endeavors and ends his days in the leper colony of San Pablo, a lost colony on the shores of the Amazon River near the Brazilian border. My intention was to keep the real name of the original model in the novel, but at a given moment the T of his last name was mysteriously changed to an F, and his name became Fushía. I made him leprous because that disease was still possible in the Amazon and because of some hair-raising pages in Flaubert's journal of his trip to the Orient, in which he gives a detailed account of his untimely encounter with a band of lepers in an Egyptian alley.

I had never seen a leper. My work as a journalist at the television station permitted me to enter the leper world in Saint Paul's hospital in Paris, where, under the pretext of writing a story, I managed to have a young doctor let me see some of the lepers and give me technical explanations about the disease. It was a common theme in all the novels located in the Amazon and, because of its rich literary tradition, had a kind of naturalistic aura about it. In order to lessen that danger somewhat, I decided not to mention the word *leprosy* even once. I remember well that I was most deeply touched when I was working on the last episode of the novel, in which Fushía, then just a vestige of a human being, chats with old Aquilino who has come to visit him after a long absence and no doubt for the last time. Never have I felt such tenderness for a character as I felt in that episode.

I planned to relate in *The Green House,* with maximum accuracy, the story of Jum, the Aguaruna cooperative, and the punishment that was inflicted on Urakusa. In the initial plan and in the first drafts of the novel, Jum appears as one of the principal characters, perhaps the most important one. But I was unable to carry out my original plan. I tried many times to reconstruct what might have been Jum's life from the time he was hurled into the world in the middle of the forest or on the bank of a river until they hung him from a tree like a manatee. And after destroying innumerable pages, I tried to narrate from his own point of view that tragic episode of his life that I knew. Every time the same thing happened. Those pages always seemed artificial, false, and awkwardly folkloric. I had already suspected it, but now I knew it in a personal and existential manner. The real truth is one thing, and the literary truth is another; and there is nothing more difficult than to want both truths to coincide.

I am not saying that literature is something totally unconnected with reality. What I am saying is that the truths that come out of literature are never the truths personally experienced by the writer or the reader. Literature is not a transposition of living experience. Real and important knowledge about reality always comes out of literature, but through lies, through a distortion of reality, through a transformation of reality by imagination and the use of words. That is why the novel that tries to depict real experience in an objective and precise way fails. It cannot succeed because the novel was invented, not to transcribe reality, but to transform it, to do something different, to make of real reality an illusion, a separate reality. When you succeed in creating something different out of real reality, real experience, you also achieve the possibility of communicating something that was not evident before that novel or poem or play existed. But you cannot plan this transmission of knowledge. The novel is a reality in itself, reality created out of fantasy and words that makes literature something very different from real life, which, of course, is something not created by imagination or words. Thus when you write a novel you must not shrink from the idea of distorting or manipulating reality. Distortion and manipulation of fact are necessary in a novel. You must lie without any scruples, but in a convincing way so that the reader accepts your lies as truths. If you succeed in this deception, something true will come through these lies, something that did not exist before, something that was not evident before. But if your intention is just to reproduce things of reality in fiction, you will probably fail as a writer because literature, in order to persuade and convince the reader, must become a sovereign world, independent, a world that has emancipated itself from its mother, from reality.

Differentiating between what is and what is not a novel comes down to whether it is possible for the text to become independent of reality, to have a life of its own. When you read *War and Peace* you have no personal experience to verify what the novel tells you, but the power of the novel is such that you are persuaded of its true reality. And so it is a novel. But if a novel, in order to be accepted and believed by the reader, demands from him a personal experience in order to verify that what is told in the book is true and convincing, it is not a novel; it is a document, disguised history, disguised journalism. For example, there was an anthropologist a few years ago who used literature in order to divulge some sociological data by writing books that were presented as novels. *The Life* by Oscar Lewis is one. It was important because it used material that was taken from real reality and was an instrument for informing the reader about that particular reality. But it is not a novel. A real novel never gives this kind of information. It can give it as a supplementary aspect of the work, but the real importance of a novel is not information; it is the creation of a different, a separate reality. Of course, the author of a novel often uses personal experience, but he transforms it into something different, into something that can be persuasive to readers from different countries, different times, different languages. This transformation that gives a work its independence from the real world, from the sources out of which it was invented or created, is what makes a work a novel.

Thus in working on *The Green House* I finally accepted the evidence at hand: I lacked the capability necessary to present the world, the abject injustices, and the other men through the eyes and the consciousness of this man whose language, customs, and beliefs escaped me. Having no choice but to reduce Jum's importance in the novel, I broke his story up into several short episodes that would be narrated, not from his point of view, but from the perspective of intermediaries and witnesses whom I could perceive much better.

The points of contact between Piura and Santa María de Nieva were, according to the plan I had for the book, Sergeant Lituma, a Mangache from Piura, assigned for a time to a military post in the jungle and later back in Piura; and Bonifacia, an Aguaruna girl educated by the nuns of Santa María de Nieva, who first becomes Sergeant Lituma's mistress, and then a prostitute of the green house with the professional name of the Jungle Lady. Suddenly, as I was polishing up the manuscript, I discovered that there was another connection, less evident but perhaps more profound, and in any case unexpected, between these two worlds.

Don Anselmo had always surprised the Piurans with his predilection for the color green; he had painted the brothel and even his harp that color. Besides had not his way of talking surprised the Piurans at first just as much? And they never managed to identify that peculiar accent of his that was neither from the coast nor from the Andes. It was one of those magical impacts that survive from time to time during the construction of a novel and which leave one amazed and happy. There was no doubt that Anselmo loved the color green because it was the color of his land. The Piurans had not been able to recognize his manner of speaking because people from the jungle never made it to Piura.

When I finished the novel in 1964, I felt unsure about myself and anxious about the book. The chapters situated in Santa María de Nieva displeased me the most. Of course, my intention had not been to write a sociological document. But I had the nagging feeling that in spite of all my efforts, I had idealized the environment and the life of the Amazon region. I decided not to publish the book until I could return to the jungle. That year I returned to Lima. This time it was not easy to reach Santa María de Nieva because of the lack of communication. Six years before I had traveled to the jungle in the Summer Institute's hydroplane. This time I traveled on my own, accompanied by a friend, an anthropologist who had been a member of the first expedition.

At first glance, hardly anything had changed in those six years; time seems not to have gone by. The authorities, the missionaries, the nuns, and the problems were the same. The rubber-and-hide business must have been even more mediocre than before because the *patrones,* the same ones who had tortured Jum and punished Urakusa, were living half-dead of hunger, almost as abandoned and miserable as the Aguarunas. We stayed at the mission and saw that, at least with respect to the system of getting pupils, some things had changed. The mission's problem now was its lack of space and teachers. It lacked room to receive all the girls who arrived from the tribes. Apparently, the natives' distrust and hostility toward the mission had ended, and now they insisted that their children be Christianized.

But the problem of what happens to the students once they leave the Mission is the same: either they return to the jungle and starve to death or enter into "civilization" as servants of the Christians. I remember as something phantasmagoric the night my friend and I spent in the cabin of one of the regional *patrones* (perhaps Arévalo Benzas or Julio Reátegui) drinking warm beer and listening to those poor devils tell us, like a humorous anecdote from the past, the tragic story of Jum. My friend and I had steered the conversation very cautiously toward that subject, but our caution was needless. With supreme naturalness, as obliging as could be, they told us everything we wanted to know, each one cutting in on the other. Their version was not different from the one we had heard six years earlier in Urakusa. They never lied nor tried to hide what had happened nor justify themselves. The only difference was that for this handful of men there was nothing incriminating about it; that is the way things were, life was just like that.

Jum was still the mayor of the village of Urakusa, and there was no way to make him remember that dark episode from his past. Besides, he gave us the impression that he felt ashamed and guilty about what had happened to him. For him and his people life had recovered its atrocious normality. They still collected hides and rubber in the forest for the same *patrones,* and their relationship with them was certainly good.

Tushía, however, had just died on his remote island in the Santiago River. Some weeks before his death, he had sent a letter, which a Jesuit showed us, to the Mission of Santa María de Nieva. I experienced an extraordinary emotion as I tried to decipher that maniacal letter scrawled in an almost incomprehensible language in which Tushía, feeling that he was about to die, asked the nuns to absolve him. He explained that he felt ill, that he was in no condition to be moved to the mission. He examined his own conscience, he confessed he was a sinner, and he claimed absolution by correspondence. Besides, he wanted them to marry him by mail. The most memorable part of that testament was that which dealt with the description of the girl, or woman, on his island he wished to marry so that there would be no confusion. In my novel, Fushía would die of leprosy. Tushía had died of something at least as spectacular—smallpox.

On returning to Paris, I made a few changes, fewer than I had feared, and the book was published in mid-1966. When it appeared, I was in Lima again trying to write another novel. One day I saw to my surprise that the newspaper *La Prensa* had published a photograph of the green house, taken sometime ago by

the journalist Elsa Arana Freyre. No longer was it the rustic little house that I remembered. It had grown and was now a modern, functional, two-story house with a luxurious garden and
no longer located in the desert. The city had grown, and the green
house was surrounded by other houses instead of sand dunes.

Not long afterward, I received an invitation to go to Piura.
Some old classmates of mine had organized an elaborate program consisting of a lecture, a visit to the San Miguel School,
and naturally a commemorative dinner at the green house. But
this is of course the beginning of another story and another novel.

⟩ 5 ⟨

Playing with Time and Language
Captain Pantoja and the Special Service

Captain Pantoja and the Special Service was my fourth novel.
I wrote it in 1972 in Barcelona, Spain, where I was living at the
time. It is a book I am very fond of because writing it was a
great change for me. It was for me the discovery of humor in
literature. Although I have always liked humor in life, until then
I was very suspicious of humor in literature. I had a great mistrust of humor in literature because I thought, quite wrongly of
course, that humor was incompatible with a literature committed to serious problems, that you could not use humor in a novel
or in a poem or in a play whose goal was to deal with serious
social, political, or historical problems.

I probably had this idea against humor because of Sartre
and the French existentialists, who had a great influence on me
during my university years. I think Sartre was a great thinker,
but he was totally humorless in his writing, in his ideas. Maybe
this mistrust of humor is something I unconsciously adopted while
reading Sartre. Humor does not really appear in my first three novels, but if it appears, it appears in spite of myself, spontaneously.

When I wrote the novel Captain Pantoja and the Special Service, called Pantaleón y las visitadoras in Spanish, I found out
that there are some stories you cannot tell in a serious way without mortally endangering them, that for some kind of material,

85

some types of stories, humor is a necessity, the only way in which you can make these stories persuasive. But it took me some time to discover this fact, which is so obvious to most writers and readers of literature.

The trip I made through the Amazon region of Peru in 1958 was very important to me because it was probably the most fertile trip I have ever made as far as my work is concerned. Some of my experiences during that trip have proved to be excellent raw material for my writing; and as I mentioned earlier, my second novel, *The Green House,* was, in a way, born out of that journey. One of the things we discovered in the small villages where we stopped was that there was great resentment on the part of the civilians, the peasants of those villages, toward the soldiers of the military garrisons. The villagers were enraged because the soldiers were always bothering the women in the villages, especially on Sundays when they had permission to go to the villages and constantly followed the women. So great was the villagers' fury that they sent letters of protest to the authorities.

That was one part of a story; the second part I would discover six years later when I returned to the same region and followed the same route. I had finished my second novel, *The Green House,* and I went there because I wanted to verify that I had not idealized the region too much in the novel. In the second journey, I discovered the second part of that story about the soldiers and the civilians in these small villages in the jungle. The civilians were still very angry at the soldiers of the garrisons, but now for a different reason. Now they were angry because they considered that the military had a privilege, that the military discriminated against them. And this privilege was something called *El Servicio de Visitadoras,* which can be translated as "The Service of Visitors." What was this service? It was a special service created by the army to send prostitutes to the military garrisons, and the civilians saw these women who came from Iquitos and from other important cities in the jungle in air force hydroplanes and in navy ships. They saw how these women went directly to the garrisons, stayed there a few days, and then went back to Iquitos, without stopping in the villages. They considered themselves victims of discrimination, which was really unacceptable.

By creating *El Servicio de Visitadoras,* the army solved one problem but created another. After having discovered this story, I started to think about the way in which the army had to proceed to create, to organize this special service of the *visitadoras.* As I had been a student in a military school and knew more or less the internal mechanisms of the army, its bureaucratic system, I began to speculate about how this special service was created.

I thought to myself that when the army decided to organize this service, it probably had to choose an officer and charge him with this mission. And how did the army choose this officer? First, it had to decide from which branch of the army he would be selected — artillery, infantry, cavalry. The most appropriate branch of the army was administration, logistics. The authorities probably had many discussions about what qualifications an officer of this kind should have so as to be able to take charge of this delicate task, and they must have reviewed the records of all available officers to find the most correct, austere, and sober one, one with great organizational skills. I decided to write a story about this officer, this man who one day suddenly received this extraordinary mission to organize a special service for the garrisons of the Amazon region.

As I had done in my previous novels, I intended to write a serious novel. Not for one moment did I have the idea of writing a humorous book. But very soon I discovered it was impossible, it was totally incompatible with the story I wanted to write to tell it in a serious way. I was constantly pushed by the material itself toward humor, toward comedy, toward grotesque or ironic or sardonic situations. It was in this practical way that I discovered that humor was in some cases a necessity, that only with humor could you create a story persuasive enough to be believed.

Thus I corrected my own feelings about the importance of humor in serious literature. This discovery was refreshing, and I wrote the book with great enthusiasm and without experiencing the difficulties and pain I always had in my previous novels or in those I wrote after *Captain Pantoja*. This novel is the only one I wrote easily. It is the only novel on which I could work many hours a day without experiencing fatigue or anguish, laughing at the same time I was writing, being amused at what was happening, at what I was telling. It was the only time that I did not feel that I was facing a difficult task, which had always been the case with everything I had previously written. I suppose the reason was that I discovered something new, and this was a refreshing experience, to have to deal with humor as a new toy.

It is difficult for me to explain why some experiences encourage me to write about or to fantasize about them and why so many other experiences fail to leave any traces in my literary work. I suppose the reason is that the experiences that are literarily fertile touch an essential aspect of my personality, something about which I am not conscious. I suppose there is a dark aspect of my personality that is deeply affected by a certain kind of experience; and then I have this urge, this impulse to fantasize about it, using that experience as a point of departure. It is true that there is an unpredictability about my work, and it intrigues me. There are constant aspects in what I have written, but there is also great diversity. But these things have not been planned. I did not write, let us say, a thriller like *Who Killed Palomino Molero?* because I thought, "Well, now, I'm going to try a thriller." No, it was because I had an idea for a story. I thought for a long time what kind of form to use for that story in order to give it more consistency and persuasiveness. Little by little I discovered that the detective story could be a form not for writing another detective story, but, as in the case of this dead language in *Pantaleón Pantoja,* to try an experiment, to try to use the structure and technique usually adopted by thriller writers to tell a different kind of story, to tell a story in which the discovery of the murder is not the essential aspect of the novel but just an accident in a novel that has another goal.

The story of the book is, of course, the story of this captain, Pantaleón Pantoja. To begin with, the name is comic; it alludes to Pantalone, the prototype character of the Italian commedia dell'arte. The story tells how this perfect officer, a model of a bureaucratic officer, very sober in his family life, and really the incarnation of the disciplined, obedient, and efficient officer, is one day called by his superiors and asked to organize this service without implicating the army in what he was doing. This service is presented to him as a secret operation, and he complies with his instructions.

But he manages to organize this service so efficiently and so cleverly that it develops into one of the most perfect and viable branches of the military organization. This, of course, starts to create new problems for the army. The service becomes a public institution and provokes the envy and resentment of the civilian population. Besides, trouble starts inside the service.

The story also tells how this institution changes Pantaleón Pantoja's personal life, how this man is so totally immersed in what he is doing that he develops a kind of chameleon psychology. To be more efficient in what he is doing, he adopts a kind of biological commitment to his work, so that in his personal life he becomes a kind of great *cafiche,* an exploiter of women, a manager of women. His personal life is totally infected, contaminated by his mission; thus in this sense he is the perfect bureaucrat of our times, totally consumed by the function he is performing, to such an extreme that he becomes just a living manifestation of this function. He organizes his personal life in such a way that it can complement and help what he does in the organization of the special service.

Little by little, the character becomes a fanatic who, in order to realize his mission, in order to implement his mission, is ready to sacrifice everything—his personal life, his family, and even the army, even this institution he loves above all else. He is so obsessed with the mission he has to accomplish that he becomes blind to everything else. We have in Spanish this proverb, *La rama que no deja ver el bosque.* I do not know that there is an English equivalent for it: "You can't see the forest for the trees." I think that is the definition of the perfect bureaucrat, the bureaucratic mind concentrated on some aspect of the world that makes him oblivious to what is happening outside the special, private parcel of that world. This situation can produce extraordinary deeds but also extraordinary catastrophes. That is true of Pantaleón. He creates an extraordinary, efficient and well-organized service, but to do that he also creates terrible problems for society, for the army, and for himself.

When I was writing *Captain Pantoja,* I went back to a part of the Amazon region, to Iquitos, the most important Peruvian city in the Amazon. I stayed there for a few days. I wanted to go into a military garrison. I wanted to know the place the women "visitors" left from when they went to the garrisons, to talk about military things, to have some idea about how the special service was organized. While I was in Iquitos, I learned that an extraordinary character had recently passed through the city, a popular preacher, someone called Hermano Francisco, Brother Francisco. He was of Brazilian origin, apparently. He had been there a few days and was very successful in his preaching. There were still some people there wearing white habits who were his followers, who had planted a big cross near a lake on the outskirts of the city, where twenty-four hours a day you could see a group of Brother Francisco's followers praying.

Many stories circulated in the city about the secret practices of this sect. Although I did not pay much attention to these stories when I was in the city because I was first of all doing research for my novel about the "visitadoras," when I left Iquitos and returned to Spain, I found I had been unconsciously considering this sect as something similar or equivalent to what Captain Pantoja was trying to build. It was then that I had the idea to counterpoint the story of the special service created by the army with the story of a religious sect that follows more or less the same path created by Pantaleón Pantoja.

I do not know whether at the beginning I had the idea that the reason for this linkage between these two institutions was that the leaders of both, in spite of the great distance between the service of prostitution and a religious sect, had in fact many things in common. First of all is this fanatical, personal vision of something, of a parcel of an activity that can push men to destruction. And that is what happened in the novel. Pantaleón Pantoja creates his service more or less at the same time that Brother Francisco, the crazy preacher, creates this fraternity, or sect, called Los Hermanos del Arca, the Ark Brotherhood. Both institutions developed and reached a kind of apogee and then declined after having been responsible for many catastrophes, including the personal catastrophe of both leaders.

In spite of the fact that, from a formal and superficial point of view, *Captain Pantoja and the Special Service* is a comic work because there are repeated comic situations and comic episodes, I think it is a very serious book. It is about the bureaucratic deformation of the mind, which I think is one of the major contemporary problems in all societies, industrialized or underdeveloped. The book deals with the problem of how specialization in life's activities can create this kind of deformation of the mind. In order to fulfill his task in an efficient and perfect way, a person finds himself secluded in a position in which he cannot see how what he does can have tragic and catastrophic repercussions and consequences in other areas or activities of society.

In establishing a separate, fictional reality, a writer of contemporary literature often uses a more debased reality than is found in real reality. But what is essential is coherence and persuasive force in that reality, which can be totally unrealistic, totally separate from our living experience. After reading certain literary works and then returning to our own real world and comparing them, we say, "This is so impossible, this is so far away from what is real." But in spite of this reaction, those books are really there and are convincing and have given me something that permits me to understand better what real life is. The major achievement for a writer is his ability to present a convincing world, a world that has only thin and remote links with real reality, a world totally born out of a profound rejection of real reality. It is true of some imaginary writers, such as Borges. The world he created is a great rejection of what real life is, of what the real world is. The real world was something unacceptable to him and he created this other world, where there are only ideas, knowledge, curiosities that deal with the intellect and in which all the material aspects of life—sex, for instance—are totally abolished, suppressed. But in spite of the fact that this world is separate from reality, it is so powerful and created with such intelligence and with such literary skill that it is totally persuasive when we read it. I doubt that Borges could have written a novel with this rejection of real reality because it would have become too artificial to be persuasive. But in a short story this can happen.

Clearly, what works well in one form does not always work well in another. My novel *Pantaleón y las visitadoras* was made into a terrible film. I do not think you can establish a norm between good books and film. Some books have been made into marvelous films, and some have been destroyed by films. The great Spanish moviemaker Luis Buñuel once told me something about this relationship that I always remember. He said that only bad novels make good films. So I have never chosen a good novel to make a film; all the novels that I have adapted to film are bad novels. It is very difficult to transform a good novel into film, but in some cases it is successful. For example, I think Orson Welles made marvelous adaptations, but he did so by taking many liberties, changing everything because cinema has its own language. To tell a story with images is quite different from telling a story with words. So you must be totally free to adapt, to change, to introduce new elements. The cinema is, like the novel, one aspect of fiction. In a film, as in a novel, you create a fiction that becomes a separate reality that must be persuasive and convincing.

As I mentioned earlier, I have never thought of form and technique in the novel as something dissociated from the story and the characters, that for me the form, which is of course essential in literature and in art in general, is always something that becomes linked to the story and is a kind of creation to make that story more convincing and persuasive. But I have to correct this statement a little bit because when I thought about writing this novel, I already had an idea of a structure for the story. I had the idea to write a story that would be only one conversation, one dialogue, a very long dialogue and a dialogue of course with distinct characteristics. My idea was not to have a realistic dialogue, but one that could be called a plural dialogue, a dialogue not limited by considerations of time and space. The dialogue could be moved freely back and forth in time, take the reader from the present to the future to the past, and then back to the present in one movement, without stops, without giving the reader the opportunity to adapt himself rationally to these shifts in time. The dialogue could also move freely from one place to another and return to the same place. I had the idea that this dialogue, in which the whole story would be concentrated, would be persuasive if from the very beginning the reader was immersed within the system in which the dialogue was constructed.

My concern was that this kind of dialogue might give the reader the impression of artificiality, of something very remote from what real life is. To overcome this problem I decided to introduce the reader to this system of dialogue little by little, in such a way that he would become accustomed to the liberties taken with time and space so slowly that he would not react critically to these movements and shifts in the story.

In the draft version of the novel, the work was only what I have just described, just one dialogue, in which the characters enter or exit and in which the story moves from one place to another and from one time to another, not following chronology, nor trying to follow a realistic displacement in space, but following only literary impulses. For instance, a character could enter the dialogue directly because he was remembered by one of the other characters who was speaking. Two characters could be talking and one of them mentions another character with whom he had a conversation a few days or weeks before. This recollection would immediately draw that character from the past and from another place into the dialogue without lengthy explanation. This shift would enable him to be perfectly integrated into the dialogue, which would then move to the past and to another place. In other cases, the dialogue would change, would move geographically because an episode that took place in another region is mentioned or remembered by the characters, and so this would immediately push the dialogue to another place. In still other situations the reasons or the mechanisms to change the evolution of the dialogue would not matter as in the examples I have just mentioned, but form — a word, for instance — used by one of the characters might immediately transfer the dialogue to another dimension or to another episode.

All this had to be established with great subtlety. It was important not to force this mechanism because I was conscious of the fact that if the reader had the impression of a pure exercise, of formal innovation, he would disbelieve what was being told in the story. I had to work out very carefully all these movements of the dialogue from one place to another or from one time to another. This aspect of the writing of the book was particularly exciting for me. I enjoyed dealing with this formal aspect of the creation of a dialogue, in which a realistic story (the story of Pantaleón Pantoja) was told in an unrealistic way, in a literary, imaginary, artificial way.

At the same time I had another idea. Ever since I wrote my first story, I have been concerned with something that every writer of short stories or novels has to deal with. This is *el lenguaje muerto* (dead language), which is always present in a novel. Unlike poetry, in which from the first word to the last you are placed in a world of extraordinary sensibility and delicacy or dynamism, a novel or a short story is a text in which it is impossible to be intense and creative all the time and to sustain vitality and dynamism in the language. When you tell a story, the moments of intensity must be supported by episodes that are purely informative, that give the reader essential information for understanding what is going on. The writer must resign himself to using a great deal of dead language for this purpose. I was bothered by this situation and asked myself why is it not possible in a novel, as in a poem, to use only intense, rich, creative language? How can I deal with this purely informative aspect of a novel, in which nothing important is happening, nothing is deeply felt by the characters, nothing is really creative? All one is left with is dead language in which, for instance, the narrator tells who is talking or where the conversation takes place.

The deadest language in a novel is the language that is inserted in the *acotaciones*. Here is a sentence that will explain what I mean. "'Do you love me?' said Jane, crossing her long legs." All the words beginning with "said Jane" are called the *acotación* in Spanish. It is a piece of information the narrator gives the reader to explain who is speaking, where she is speaking and what she is doing when speaking. Maybe that she has long legs has some interest; but in general in a novel or short story, the text that comes between the dashes (we use the dash in Spanish; I do not think you use this dash in English) is dead language, purely informative language in which you rarely introduce something new, creative, or important. If you use much dialogue in a novel or short story, you have to face this problem. How to give or use this necessary information in such a way that the language can be less pedestrian, or *terre à terre?*

I had this idea, or this temptation, to write a story in which the *acotaciones* could be used so that this text would become as important for the realization of the novel as the essential part of the dialogue, in which what is really important is established or mentioned.

I had many ideas, and what I finally accomplished did not come suddenly or easily but was the result of a long process. In the end, what I did was this. I used the *acotaciones* to present all necessary description in the novel. Again, the novel was just a conversation in which the characters speak among themselves in a plural dialogue without limitations of space and time. But the narrator uses the *acotaciones* to introduce not only information about who is speaking and where but also to give much more information about the place, about the time, about what other people are doing at the moment or before or after, as well as introduce all the necessary background of the story—that is, social, economic, and political descriptions of the country and society.

I had the idea that by this device the dead language would be less dead, would be more alive in the story, that this could change the very nature of the *acotaciones*. And that is finally what I did in *Captain Pantoja and the Special Service*. I used this mechanism in a very slow rhythm in order to familiarize the reader with this system. The system was divided into two different formulas. One was to move the dialogue freely in space and time; the other, to introduce inside the dialogue, as part of the dialogue itself, all the information that is usually separated from the dialogue in the conventional or normal novel. Now here I need to explain something, to say something parenthetically about time.

Time is an essential aspect of fiction that gives it a separate identity, a personality that is different from the real reality. For obvious reasons time in a novel is never like time in real life. This is true even in the most realistic novel, in the novel that succeeds in imitating life. In a novel, time always has a beginning and an end. It never flows as it does in real life. In a novel, because you have to tell how different characters are acting or moving or thinking, you are obliged to stop in order to differentiate the characters, actions, and episodes. Thus you are forced to break the movement that time has in reality, and so you are always introducing an artificial time in a novel. This artificial time always occurs in the modern novel, in which authors are much more self-conscious of what they do with the creation of time structures than in the classical novels of the eighteenth and nineteenth centuries, when novelists did not really care about these problems in a theoretical way. They did not think about the creation of different structures, the structures of reality. Probably many classical novelists were convinced that when they wrote their novels they were imitating reality, not only in the words they used, but also in the creation of time movements in the stories.

In fact, in any novel, when you investigate how time evolves, how the story flows, you discover that there is a creation, a time structure, that is in most cases a distinctive quality of each author, of each fictitious work. An essential aspect of the originality of a novelist, a narrator, is the way in which he creates these time structures in his work. In Faulkner's novels, for example, time has been created with great care and extraordinary skill so that it functions in the creation of atmosphere, in the creation of the ambiguities and subtleties of the story. The way in which the narrator moves in time and the way in which the action of the novel goes back and forth in time are essential to the realization of the story. The manipulation of time occurs in all novels. In some, it is more obvious; in many others, it is almost invisible. And so if you search for the time structure in a novel, you will discover that it is one of the aspects of the novel's originality and also one of the aspects in which all novels differ from and remain at a distance from the model, which is reality, real reality.

In *Captain Pantoja and the Special Service* you have to think of time as something similar to space. Time has a quality that is material, exactly as does space. Time is something that exists, with a beginning and an end, and also with a material quality, with a material nature; thus the narrator can move the story in time in the same way that he moves the story in space. The story can move freely from the past to the future and from the future to the past because time is there like space, in which nothing is lost, nothing has vanished. Time is there. The past is like the future or like the present, a stage to which you can move back anytime you wish. If time has this spatial quality, this territorial quality, you can fragment time, you can divide it, giving it the structure of a biological being, of a biological entity. In my plays these time structures are also exceedingly important. In at least one play, the time structures become the essence of the whole work, what the work is about. I think it started with *Captain Pantoja,* for it was when I wrote that book that I became fascinated with this formal possibility. One of the reasons why literature is important is that it gives us an instrument with which to understand time. In real life time is something that devours us, is something that does not give us the necessary perspective to understand how this time in which we are immersed flows; and so we do not have perspective, we do not have the necessary distance to understand really what is happening. Therefore, we need artificial order for understanding time.

One of the major contributions of literature in our lives is that it establishes an artificial order of the world, of time, of space, of the living experience. Particularly the great works, the masterworks of literature, are instruments that permit us to adapt ourselves to this *vorágine,* to this vortex that real life is, that real living experience is. When you explore the possibilities of creating a time structure in a story, you are not only doing something that is an artificial achievement and the achievement of a formal skill, the mastery of language, or the mastery of techniques to hypnotize the reader. You are also creating an instrument through which we can better understand how daily experience, living experience, is happening in reality. And so this fascination with time, which is a distinct characteristic of modern literature, is not gratuitous, not artificial. It is a way of reacting to a reality in which we feel ourselves — particularly in contemporary societies — totally lost. We are becoming so insignificant, so minor in this extraordinary and impersonal world, which is the world of modern societies, that we need a way to place ourselves in it. This artificial organization that literature gives to life is something that helps us in real life to feel less lost and confused.

Again, in modern literature time and structure are something about which writers are very conscious, unlike classical novelists. Cervantes or Dickens or Hawthorne probably never thought about the creation of a time structure in a novel, but that does not mean they did not create time structures, and very complex and original ones, in their novels. For the classical novelists, creation of time structures came about in a spontaneous way, by instinct, by intuition. They thought they were dealing with moral problems, for instance; they thought that moral problems were really the essential problems in a novel. But at the same time, in a practical way, they were dealing with the same problems as the contemporary novelist. When you write a story you have to create a structure, a different structure in the eighteenth century than in the twentieth. But you need a structure, you need to use the language in such a way that the story can be convincing to the reader. You must use some tricks, some techniques, give some facts while you hide others, in order to create a literary structure. The classic novelists were not aware of these requirements, or at least they did not use a language that gave evidence of their awareness. The first novelist in the nineteenth century who became conscious of these purely formal and technical problems of the novel was Flaubert. With Flaubert the novel appeared for the first time not only as a moral task or the creation of a story but also as a purely technical problem, the problem of the creation of a convincing language and the organization of time and also the problem of the function of the narrator in the novel. In the past, probably very few writers were concerned about the techniques and form of the novel as something dissociated from the story itself.

You can do what I have done in *Captain Pantoja and the Secret Service* — use the *acotaciones* of the novel to give the reader information periodically that enlightens him about the context of what is going on in the dialogue. In the novel this is done, as I said, very slowly. At the beginning, the dialogue has the same realistic appearance as a conventional work. Pantaleón talks with his wife, explaining that he has an appointment with his superiors in which he will receive a new mission, and his wife is very excited with the prospect of staying in the capital, in Lima. The information given by the narrator in the "acotaciones" is sparse, specific, and concrete.

But little by little this material starts to change. In the dialogue more and more information is introduced in the "acotaciones," and the reader slowly becomes accustomed to seeing in these explanatory comments of the narrator a source of information that gradually becomes dissociated from what is going on in the dialogue among the characters. For instance, when the system is developed to its maximum possibility, a dialogue may start in which one character asks another: "Do you love me?" Then the reader is given information about who is speaking, what he did before he started to speak, and what he will do before this conversation will have finished. For instance, he will take a plane and go from Iquitos to Lima, to the capital, and in the capital he will have three meetings with three different generals to whom he will explain what he is doing in Iquitos. Then he will take another plane and return to Iquitos and will kiss his wife. Then this phrase, which started here, will finish.

At that moment in the novel the reader is supposed to be so familiar with the system that he will not feel shocked or disconnected because he is, by now, accustomed to move in time and space, not for chronological, rational, or realistic reasons, but only for the literary necessities of the story. He will be totally accustomed to move in this world as in a different world, a world that has nothing to do with the real world, a world that has its own mechanisms, its own reasons, its own nature.

This treatment of time and space was another aspect of this novel that was especially exciting for me because it was an experiment that explored a possibility of the narrative form to an extreme. I have perspective enough to know that when I started this I had already tried unconsciously to use this kind of time structure in my previous novel. When I discussed my first novel, *The Time of the Hero,* I mentioned the dialogue at the end of the novel in which for the first time I used these "vasos comunicantes" in this way. Mixed in with one dialogue was a second dialogue that was held in a different place and in a different time. The two dialogues were interwoven, without the reader being given any explanation.

I think that this structure of *Captain Pantoja* is an evolution from something I started to do when I wrote my first novel, at least fifteen years before. The difference is that when I wrote *Captain Pantoja* I was totally conscious of what I was doing with time. In my first novel this use of time was more nearly spontaneous than a conscious decision. As I mentioned earlier, in the draft my idea was that this plural dialogue would be the total structure of the novel; but when I finished the draft of the second version, I felt that it was not convincing. I felt that this structure, only a dialogue with these explanatory comments introduced within the dialogue, was not sufficient to create the impression of totality that is essential in a novel if it is going to succeed in giving the reader the impression of a total, self-sufficient world. I felt that something was lacking there, and so I introduced other chapters, chapters that alternate with the dialogues, chapters in which I also used dead language, that is, language made not with creative words but with stereotypes or clichés.

Even as a young boy, I was fascinated with popular genres, popular artistic genres—soap operas, comics, "novelas por entregas," that is, serial novels. What is characteristic of these popular genres is the stereotypes, the images or the language used in a stereotypical way, not in a creative way. There is nothing original; on the contrary, the authors of these popular genres resort to the stereotype, to the cliché, because that is what the popular genre is about. I have always had the temptation, even years before I wrote *Captain Pantoja,* to use some forms of popular genres, but creatively, using these stereotypes so as to rejuvenate them, revitalize them, by giving them a different function without destroying their nature as stereotypes.

That is what I did in the alternate chapters of *Captain Pantoja.* I introduced documents, for instance the military reports that Pantaleón writes to his superiors explaining what is going on in the service he is organizing. This is dead language, of course; it is the language of stereotypes. I remember very well in military school all those incredible documents we had to write or read. The language was so stereotyped that it gave you an idea of something totally disconnected from what real life is. For instance, I always remember the first chapter of the rules of an officer: "*Las órdenes deben ser obedecidas sin dudas ni murmuraciones*" (Orders must be obeyed without questioning or verbal complaints). That is what I mean by stereotyped language or dead language. All such documents have stereotyped language.

What Captain Pantoja is talking about in these reports is so far removed from the usual subject matter of reports of this kind that the language assumes a different function and a different meaning. In his reports, Pantoja talks to his superiors using all these clichés, all these tricks of language generally used to discuss military maneuvers or logistics problems of a battalion. To talk about prostitutes and how they are performing creates a kind of contradiction that, I hoped, might give this dead language a new personality, a new vitality, a dynamism. The chapters in which these documents are exposed to the reader without any explanation from the narrator are the most humorous episodes in the novel.

Other documents are used, for instance journalistic texts, some articles apparently from a local newspaper, in which the problems that the Special Service provoked in the civilian population are described. Also used are scripts from a radio broadcaster in Iquitos who likes to exaggerate, a kind of tropical journalist, very primitive, who is really an incarnation of the stereotypical mind, a mind that moves only among stereotypes, totally incapable of saying or creating anything original. But my hope was that in the context of the novel this dead language could change its nature and become literary language.

From the point of view of the novel, literary language is any language that has the capacity to take the reader from real reality and move him to a fictitious reality, to a separate reality. Any kind of language that has the ability to do that is a literary language. Establishing and using a literary language is the goal of the novel, what the novel must achieve in order to be a novel. The characteristics of literary language cannot be specified because any kind of language can perform these functions if the writer has the ability to use it well. You can use a sophisticated language or a plain language; in some cases you can use stereotyped language or a creative language; you can be baroque or simple; you can use humor. You can use any kind of language, but always in a context in which there is total coherence. That is essential in a novel. Also essential in a novel is a purpose that goes beyond the purely formal. You can be a formalist, someone who is fascinated with experimentation in language or in structure; but if this experiment is your main concern, you will not create a truly separate reality. Concern for language or structure must be subordinated to a purpose, which is this creation of a different society. That is the reason why in many cases contemporary experimental literature fails to produce great literature. For instance, the "nouveau roman" in France. It was an interesting movement. Its writers created new forms and techniques, but these elements were their only concerns. It seems to me that they have not really produced one masterwork. The nouveau roman is vanishing because it is purely formal. Literature, in spite of the fact that it is always formal, cannot be only form because in the end it becomes dead language.

As you can see, in spite of the fact that it is a humorous and comic novel, *Captain Pantoja and the Special Service* is also an experimental book, a book in which I consciously experimented with form. I think it is probably the book in which I have been most conscious of form, of the purely technical aspects of the creation of the novel. Of course, form is essential and form is what takes much of your time when you write a novel. But in most cases an author deals with form incidentally, more by intuition than by rational decision. My rational decision to experiment and explore the possibilities of form in *Captain Pantoja* has not always been understood by critics, who have devoted much more attention, for instance, to the technical aspects of my other books and have given *Captain Pantoja* more the character of just light entertainment. This is not so. In *Captain Pantoja* I worked as much as in my other books and probably tried harder to experiment and accomplish something creatively in the purely technical or formal aspect of the story.

◆ 6 ◆

From Soap Opera to Serious Art
Aunt Julia and the Scriptwriter

When I discussed the writing of *Captain Pantoja and the Special Service,* I explained how I discovered humor in literature, how I became enthusiastic over the possibilities of humor in serious literature. This discovery was very important for writing the book *Aunt Julia and the Scriptwriter* because if I had not already written *Captain Pantoja, Aunt Julia* would have been a very different book from what it actually is. I also discussed the fascination I have always had for popular genres, for those artistic or semiartistic genres that reach the masses, as for example, the feuilleton of the nineteenth century, in which novels were serialized in newspapers for the entertainment of the general reader. Something really extraordinary happened with this popular genre in the nineteenth century. It was one of those rare occasions in which a popular genre, an artistic genre with great appeal for the masses, was at the same time a very creative and original artistic achievement. You know that the best prose writers in the nineteenth century, the great creators, were at the same time popular writers who wrote books and stories that reached all kinds of audiences. That was the case in France; that was the case in England and Spain. Writers like Victor Hugo, Alexandre Dumas, and Charles Dickens were great creators, original writers, and at the same time they managed to write the sort of book that could satisfy simultaneously the sophisticated reader, the intellectual reader, and the average reader—even the primitive reader and the elementary reader, who were interested only in the anecdote or the episodes of a story.

This link between a popular genre and a creative artist has been present on only a few occasions in history, as in the novels of chivalry in the Middle Ages. Although novels of chivalry were a popular genre, they were also, in many cases, artistic achievements, marvelous books of narrative, that were appreciated by all sections of society. For instance, in Spain we have this extraordinary novel called *Tirant lo Blanch,* or *Tirante lo Blanco* in Spanish.[1] From a very early age, I was fascinated with this possibility of creative literature that could also be popular. As you know this is not the case in modern times. Creative literature is sophisticated literature that is usually only for the elite, the intellectual elite. And there is popular literature that is not artistic, that is stereotyped and mechanical; for example, the soap opera, which is a continuation of the feuilleton tradition of the nineteenth century and the novel of chivalry of the Middle Ages only in the sense that it is written to accommodate the tastes of the general audience; it does not satisfy a more sophisticated audience.

I always had the temptation to use the mechanics, the techniques, and the themes of popular genres as raw material for writing an artistic work, in which clichés and dead language could change its nature because of the context in which they were used. I tried to do something like that in *Captain Pantoja and the Special Service* when I used fake documents, newspaper articles, and scripts for the radio programs of one of the characters, Sinche. In that novel I used stereotypes of the journalistic jargon; and

1. *Tirant lo Blanch* (1490). Famous Catalan novel of chivalry, the first three parts of which were written by Johanot Marturell and the fourth by Martí Johán de Galba. The work was translated into Spanish in 1515.

through the context in which these documents were incorporated, I tried to give this kind of language a different substance, a different perspective.

Aunt Julia and the Scriptwriter is also organized with this intention. Again, my idea was to write a novel with stereotypes, with clichés, with all the instruments of the popular novel, the soap opera, and the radio serial, but in such a way that these elements could be transformed into an artistic work, into something personal and original. As in all my books, the idea came to me from a personal experience. In the mid-fifties, when I was a student in Lima, I worked as a journalist in a radio station. There I met an extraordinary character, a Bolivian, who wrote all the soap operas for a radio station called Radio Central, which was owned by the same person who owned the station where I worked. I was immediately fascinated by this man. He was more than a scriptwriter, more than a soap-opera writer. He was really an industry of soap operas because he wrote practically all the serials that were broadcast by Radio Central. I do not know how many, but he did quite a few each day. He wrote all the scripts and had this amazing facility for producing these stories, which were probably the same story with different names, with different characters living in different places. He was also the director and acted in all the serials.

I was fascinated by him because of this facility of his, because of this naïveté with which he did something that for me, who at that time was thinking of becoming a serious writer one day, seemed so difficult and so serious. To be a writer was extremely important to me; and I think this Bolivian was the first professional writer I had ever met. At that time in Peru, in 1953–54, there were no professional writers, I mean people who dedicated their whole life to writing. That was unthinkable. You could not make a living out of writing. And so writers were lawyers or teachers or journalists, who wrote only on Sundays and when they had holidays. But this Bolivian, no; he was only a writer.

His time was devoted just to writing, and he could make a living out of it. At the same time he was very popular. He was a writer, probably the only writer in Peru who really reached an enormous audience. All kinds of people were fascinated with the soap operas of Radio Central.

At the same time he was like a caricature of what a writer was for me because he was not interested in serious literature. I think he rarely read a book. Although I do not think I ever heard the serials that this Bolivian wrote and directed and acted in himself, I was fascinated by this man, and something happened to him that gave me the idea for writing a story using his case. What happened to him was that he suffered from *surmenage* (exhaustion or overwork). He worked so hard that it was not surprising that he became exhausted. Apparently, Radio Central started to receive calls from the public protesting the inaccuracies and contradictions they found in the soap operas. Memory is mischievous; it changes things. It transforms to fiction the objective event, the objective world. And so I am not entirely sure that what I am telling you now is exactly what happened. I may be using my own fiction as an objective recollection. I try to be objective, but I am not sure I can be. I do not know whether the inaccuracies were really grotesque. They were certainly not as grotesque as they were in my novel. But Radio Central did receive calls from the public saying, "We can't understand the story; there are inaccuracies. There are contradictions."

This was for me an extraordinary incentive for imagining a story in which a writer, a writer like this Bolivian, a writer of soap operas, became so prolific that one day he started mixing up the different stories in his mind. This was an extremely appealing idea to me, and ever since then I thought about writing a novel or short story about a writer of soap operas who was as popular and successful as the Bolivian who had this grotesque tragedy. One day he was so immersed in this imaginary world that the boundaries of his different soap operas started to vanish, and the parts of his fictitious world mixed one with the other.

That was my first idea for the novel. I completely lost touch with this man. I went to Europe, where I lived for many years. But this idea for a novel or short story stayed with me.

It was only after having written *Captain Pantoja and the Special Service,* after I had discovered humor in literature and attempted to use the techniques of popular genres, that a possible shape for the story of the scriptwriter of soap operas came to me. I decided to write a novel. I wanted to write a novel in which the story of Pedro Camacho would develop before the reader through the internal process of the deterioration of this Bolivian's soap operas. The soap operas would be presented directly to the reader; and by reading Pedro Camacho's soap operas, the reader would follow this process of deterioration of the mind of this writer who is, let us say, submerged and destroyed by his characters, by his imagination. Of course, I could not reproduce Pedro Camacho's soap operas, even fictitiously. And so I invented a form in which the soap operas were not reproduced as I had reproduced the newspaper articles or el Sinchi's scripts in *Pantoja* but were given in a kind of synopsis of Pedro Camacho's original scripts.

There were two different levels of narration in my idea of the novel. The first level was Pedro Camacho's original scripts. These scripts would not be known to the reader. On a second level these soap operas were transmuted and converted into a synopsis, told by an impersonal narrator from an ironic perspective. This would be the material exposed to the reader. The technical incentive for me was to develop a writing in which these synthesized soap operas of Pedro Camacho would deteriorate internally. The reader would perceive at the beginning, subtly and subliminally, that something had started to go wrong in these stories. There would be inaccuracies, there would be contradictions. Little by little this process would increase. Characters would jump from one story to another. People who were old in one chapter would be young in the next chapter. Or the reverse. Things like that. The reader would understand that all this confusion was a manifestation, a symptom of what was happening to the mind of the author of the stories. In this way, the real story of the novel, which was the story of the soap-opera writer Pedro Camacho, would appear, would become evident to the reader.

That was my first idea and that was also the draft version, the first version of the book. But when I had written some chapters, I became worried. I felt that the novel was becoming more and more an experiment. The novel had for me the appearance of an experiment in writing. It was like an exercise of style. As I said in my discussion of *The Time of the Hero,* I have always had a realistic obsession; I need to give the impression, the feeling, that a novel has serious and deep links with a living experience, with real life. I have never written fantastic literature, not because I am against it; on the contrary I greatly admire this kind of literature. But when I write, I need a linkage with living reality, which is also an appearance, as in the case of fantastic literature. But I feel more at ease writing a book that simulates reality than writing a book that simulates unreality. For me it is easier to invent, to produce persuasive fiction if it has the appearance of being realistic.

When I was writing the first version of *Aunt Julia and the Scriptwriter,* I suddenly felt that that was not the case with this work, that all this was happening at such a level of sophistication and artificiality that the reader would have the idea, not of a realistic novel, but of a kind of joke or purely experimental book. I did not like that effect and decided to change my idea of the novel. It was at that time, at that moment, that I decided to alternate the story of Pedro Camacho, the soap-opera writer, with another story, a story that would convey realistic nature in an obvious and direct manner. I decided to experiment. I thought, why not introduce myself in the novel as a character?

Why not use my own name, my own face, my own biography as the realistic counterpoint of this incredible and unrealistic story of Pedro Camacho? Why not put myself as an anchor in reality, an autobiographical document, something that is obviously so realistic, my own life? It was this balance that would give this incredible world of absurd fantasies, which is the soap-opera world of Pedro Camacho, a context profoundly rooted in reality.

I remembered that during those years in Lima in which the Bolivian was writing soap operas, incredible stories and melodramatic stories, I myself was the protagonist of a kind of soap opera. At that time I was eighteen and had married for the first time a woman twelve years older than myself. This marriage had created a big scandal in my family; this grotesque marriage was like a story taken from a soap opera. And so I said why not try to introduce that episode of my life into the novel, but exactly as it happened, as a document, not as fiction, something that would be exactly the reverse, the antipode of Pedro Camacho's soap opera. The quest for the marriage license in *Aunt Julia* is probably 80 percent autobiographical. Julia, my first wife and to whom this book is dedicated, and I had a problem getting a marriage license in Chincha. Nobody wanted to marry us because I had not reached my majority. The legal age for getting a license is now eighteen; at that time it was twenty-one. And so we had a lot of trouble, and all this now seems comical. But in the book I added many anecdotes, many elements. A soap opera of Pedro Camacho, by its very personality and nature, has to be completely cut off from real experience, from real life, because what happens in a soap opera is something that is a caricature of real life. (In Pedro Camacho's imagination, he is himself a caricature as a writer; and so I made him a caricature physically, a dwarfish man.) I would balance this absurd world with a document on real life.

I would use two different languages. One language that would be, as soap operas usually are, very sophisticated, comically elegant; the soap-opera script is usually written in pretentious language, language that pretends to be literary. I thus made a caricature of a caricature in the soap operas of Pedro Camacho. I tried to write a language in which the caricature of the caricature would convert the dead language of a soap opera into a living language. I was very excited doing that. I wanted to alternate this language with a factual language, a language in which the event would be transmitted as if in a perfect report, in an article in a newspaper, as a document.

I started a second version of the novel in which I alternated the story of this young writer, who was myself at that time, with the soap operas of Pedro Camacho. It was a very instructive experience for me as a writer because it was the only time in which I have tried to be totally truthful in writing a novel, in which I have tried not to invent but to remember and report my recollections objectively. I discovered it was impossible, that you cannot do this if you are writing a novel, that fiction is incompatible with objective reporting of living experience, that there is an essential incompatibility between these two things—fiction and a living document, an objective report of real life. I was constantly misguided by my own memory. My own memory was being deformed by my imagination, by my fantasy. I felt there was an invincible pressure from my fantasy to introduce changes in my memory in order to have a better document, in order to improve the text I was writing. On the other hand what I was trying to remember and put in the novel was not put in a vacuum but in a novel in which there was an imaginary context, a fantasy world, the world of Pedro Camacho.

This context also exercised a tremendous pressure on the document, urging changes in order to establish a continuity, to establish something that could give the story a more convincing, a more persuasive shape. I also discovered that when you write a novel there is nothing that can really be called factual writing, factual style. You have to choose words, you have to select among different possibilities. This selection introduces an imaginary element in the writing that is fatal. There is no way to avoid it, even if you decide to write in a transparent style, even if you want the prose to be totally invisible and to put the matter directly to the reader. This is a choice, usually a sophisticated, complex choice, in which invisibility can only be attained through complexity, through a technique that is extremely subtle and drawn out.

Thus the language was factual only when it was especially literary, only when it was artificial. This also changed remembrance. I think this has been the most educative, the most pedagogical experience I have ever had as a writer. I fought against myself in writing this version of the novel, trying to combine fantasy with personal biography, an imaginary world with a documented world. I discovered it was impossible. And so I resolved once again to change the shape, the outlook of the novel.

The book in its final form presents two different worlds, two different levels of reality. One level, the world of soap operas, the world of an imagination that is mechanically using stereotypes, clichés, and following a pattern that is more or less the pattern of popular narrative genres is transmitted in the novel as a caricature of a caricature in order to give this dead language a literary dimension. The other level, through the language of documents, appears to present an objective world in which a young narrator who usurps my name remembers an episode of his life.

When I discovered that I could not really be objective, I introduced many changes, as I mentioned earlier; and so these parts of *Aunt Julia and the Scriptwriter* are not exactly autobiographical episodes. I used many personal reminiscences, and the general outline of the event that Varguitas tells in the book is more or less autobiographical; but the added episodes and anecdotes are also numerous, and probably the imaginary factor in these objective episodes in *Aunt Julia and the Scriptwriter* is just as recurrent as in the soap operas of Pedro Camacho. On the other hand in Pedro Camacho's soap operas I also introduced many personal elements, sometimes deliberately and sometimes not.

My idea was not to make contrasts in the novel between two forms of literature—serious literature and popular literature—two ways of approaching the literary vocation. But I discovered when finishing this version of the novel that in fact I had done so, that the contrasts between the two worlds, the objective world and the imaginary world, were also matched by these two different attitudes. In one case we have a young Peruvian who tries to become a writer, who considers literature as the most important thing in the world and sees literature as a very serious responsibility not only from an intellectual point of view but also from a moral point of view, as a moral commitment. In the other case we have this other man, for whom literature is just a profession, just craftsmanship, something that he knows how to do and does very well, but without any kind of moral commitment or sense of moral responsibility. I do not know if at the same time or afterwards or maybe previously I became concerned with this problem, which I consider a serious problem of our time, this divorce between popular literature, literature for mass consumption, and creative literature, literature created in an original way and used as an instrument to create something new and, at the same time, as a means to understand better the world and human experience.

It is not true that the difference between a soap-opera writer and an artistic writer is that a soap-opera writer writes for money and an artistic writer writes only for glory. No. Many artistic writers also write for money, and writers of soap operas sometimes write for glory and artistic achievement. I think the difference is the difference that Roland Barthes made between *écrivante* and *écrivain (escribiente y escritor)*. If I remember, he said an *écrivante* is someone who uses language only as an instrument, an instrument through which a message, any sort of message, can be transmitted. And an *écrivain,* a writer, is someone who uses language as an end in itself, as something that in itself has justification. That is a good distinction between a professional, or instrumental, writer and a creative writer. If in writing you find your recompense, reward, satisfaction, and justification for your efforts, doing what you are doing regardless of the outcome, then you are a creative writer. But if you have craftsmanship and use it in order to produce an effect—political or religious propaganda or some kind of social statement—then you are perhaps a scriptwriter. Some scriptwriters are very efficient, have great craftsmanship, and can write marvelous soap operas or marvelous scripts for just about anything. For this purpose craftsmanship is much more important than inspiration, obsession, or personal testimony. The boundary between them is subtle. It is clear in extreme cases, but more confused in those cases in which the writer encompasses characteristics from both sources. For a specific example, executives of a Venezuelan TV channel decided one day to hire good writers, important writers, so as to improve the artistic quality of their soap operas. They hired Salvador Garmendia and Adriano González León, both novelists, both good writers. Garmendia and González León wrote what is called in Venezuela *culebrones* (soap operas). They were total failures, catastrophes. The public was not interested. The station had to stop the serials. The novelists could not write soap operas; they were totally inept at the task.

A serious writer is someone who is able to distort reality out of a personal obsession or personal belief, and to present this distortion in such a persuasive way that it is perceived by the reader as an objective description of reality, of the real world. This is what achievement in art and literature is. A good scriptwriter of soap operas is also someone who distorts reality, not out of a personal obsession or personal vision, but out of the stereotypes that are established in society. That is also a meaningful difference between the two forms of writing. An isolated incident that is reported by a newspaper is something that you can compare with or differentiate from your own experience of the rest of reality. But in a novel this incident should always have a relationship with everything that happens, and if there is a real correspondence it becomes a vision more than a description. There are writers like Alexandre Dumas, a genius, in whom it is difficult to establish these differences. His personal vision was so close to what society really was that his work represents an extraordinary combination of personal achievement and the kind of institutionalized literature that he wrote. He wrote serious, artistic, original literature, and at the same time he was a mechanical writer who produced much stereotyped literature. And there is Corín Tellado. She is a Spanish writer of soap operas, probably the most widely read writer in the Spanish-speaking world, much more so than García Márquez, although her popularity has declined in recent years. She has a genius for writing soap operas for TV and radio and serials in magazines. In the 1950s in Peru she was read by everybody. I interviewed her for my TV program and was fascinated by her. She is a Spaniard from Asturias who has always lived in small towns in the provinces—never in Madrid or other big cities. She has dedicated her life to writing, and she publishes two novels monthly. At the same time she writes scripts for TV and radio. She is like Pedro Camacho—not an artist but a genius in a productive way.

From a cultural point of view the richest moments in civilization, in history, have occurred when the boundaries separating popular and creative literature disappear, and literature becomes simultaneously both things—something that enriches all audiences, something that can satisfy all kinds of mentalities and knowledge and education, and at the same time is creative and artistic and popular. Dickens, Hugo, and Dumas are extraordinary cases in point; and in Spain in the nineteenth century there are many other examples, such as Pérez Galdos.

Aunt Julia and the Scriptwriter is a novel in which the separation of literature and the popular genres is an important element of the work. The young writer is fascinated with this man who is a real writer, the only writer he knows who at the same time is not only a caricature but an essential negation of what he considers literature to be, an artist to be, a writer to be. Why is this so? Why does this divorce exist? Is it a product of modernity or is it an individual choice? Is the public—the readers and the audience—responsible for this divorce? Of course, there is no one answer in the novel, but I think it appears as a recurrent and constant background to what is happening in the book.

Humor is also important in *Aunt Julia and the Scriptwriter*. Not the kind of humor that I used in *Captain Pantoja and the Special Service,* where it is something rough and vulgar and very direct. In this novel humor is much more indirect and subtle and results from a context in which it is the reader who has to convert what is in the book into a comic experience.

From a formal point of view I had one big challenge in the novel. In the soap operas of Pedro Camacho I did not want to be purely artificial. The idea was not for soap operas to be there only to express or manifest the psychological crisis of the soap-opera writer. No. That was one function of the soap operas. But the other function, equally important, was that the soap operas be there as stories in themselves, stories that could attract, fascinate, and hypnotize the reader as fiction should. But the problem was that these soap operas, because they had to convey this other story, the story of its author, had limitations. These stories could not have a beginning or an end because through them I had to show what was happening to this writer's mind through its deterioration and gradual confusion. And so these stories could have a beginning, but they could not have an end. They had to be mixed and integrated one with the other.

How was I to construct the stories to be persuasive stories and at the same time only chapters of this great chaos that the novel would present to the reader in the final collapse of the imagination, of the imaginary world of Pedro Camacho? I tried different ways and finally found this device that is a great question mark at the end of all the soap operas, something that is not exactly the end, something that never closes the story but gives the reader all the possible ends for each story. In every serial this is exactly what happens at the end of each chapter. The script should have an intriguing element that can awaken the curiosity of the reader or the audience to what is going to occur next.

At the same time in all these soap opera endings, I wanted to provoke the reader's curiosity about the future development of the story and also give him the possibility of deciding on an ending for the story, which would give it the shape of a real story, with a beginning and an end. The story endings were the most difficult aspect of writing this novel. I worked very, very hard. The last paragraphs in each Pedro Camacho chapter were written many times, with different versions, and in the end I think it is the part of the novel with which I am most satisfied, or the least dissatisfied. The way in which the soap operas end in the novel is probably my best achievement in writing this book.

I am surprised at what has happened to *Aunt Julia and the Scriptwriter* because I thought this novel would be understood only by Peruvian readers. It is a book in which there are so many allusions and references to Peruvian habits and customs, to Peruvian institutions and Peruvian rituals, as well as so many references to the 1950s in Peru—the music, what the people read at that time—that I did not think the novel would be of interest to foreign audiences. That has proved to be one of my great surprises as a writer because this novel has been probably more successful abroad than any of my other works. Even in countries having the kind of stereotypes the radio serials represented, people have recognized something to which they could easily refer in their own reality, in their own society. This shows how broad this phenomenon of the soap-opera mentality, of the soap-opera language, the soap-opera institution, really is; how in all cultures, in all countries, developed or underdeveloped, this kind of parallel culture or parallel literature represented by the soap opera is a contemporary phenomenon, a contemporary institution.

In spite of the fact that soap operas are such a distortion of real life, of reality, these melodramas have more influence in real life—at least more visible influence on the attitudes of the people—than creative literature. Radio and television serials have a tremendous impact on the way people think, act, and function in life. Therefore, it can be said that in Latin America, in Peru, the literature that is most representative of real life, of real reality, is not creative literature—the great achievement of the intellect—but the popular genres. These popular genres, in their distortion, in their stereotyped report of life, are also closer to what real life is than creative, artistic literature. That is why achievements in art or literature must not be judged by comparing them with reality. "Dynasty" or "Dallas" or "El derecho de nacer" (in Peru in the 1950s an incredible radio soap opera, incredible because it was so popular) is probably closer not only to what people want but to what people are. I do not know what conclusion to draw from this assessment; but I think it is true, and that it accounts for the appeal that soap operas have for enormous audiences, who easily identify themselves with something that is representative of what they are, at least in a symbolic way, in a psychological way.

In preparing to write *Aunt Julia and the Scriptwriter,* I did not listen to soap operas. For ideas I did not need to hear or watch soap operas, but only to look inside myself. As a writer one of my problems is that I have many projects and not enough time to have them all materialize. I know that I will never have enough time to write all the stories I want to write. In addition, I have always had a secret perversion—a fascination with melodrama, grotesque stories of adventure, the distortion of reality that melodrama represents. I am deeply sensitive to this literary perversion. And so in this novel I found a way to solve both problems. I used several of my projects, any one of which could have become a novel, for the stories in *Aunt Julia,* using Pedro Camacho as a pretext in a melodramatic style.

I am pleased with the translation of *Aunt Julia and the Scriptwriter.* I think Helen Lane did a good job. We worked closely together, and she understood all of the subtleties of the language. She worked very hard to create the two different kinds of language in the novel, one for the soap operas and one for the young narrator. There are mistakes, of course. Recently, someone pointed out a serious mistake in one of the phrases. But this is inevitable. The important thing in a translation is that the translator really re-create in his own language what I have done in Spanish. Unfortunately, I have had very sad experiences with translations. Sometimes, even if I am consulted, it is difficult to help a translator, for instance in a language completely foreign to me. For example, there is a funny but also sad anecdote about my first novel, *La ciudad y los perros,* being translated into Swedish. One day a friend of mine, a Spaniard who lived in Stockholm and knew Swedish, told me that each time the young cadets of the military school smoked in the novel, they smoked marijuana. I said, "What? There is not one marijuana cigarette in my novel." I think I know what happened. Because terrifying things continually occur in the novel, the translator probably thought that the cigarettes smoked by the cadets should also reflect that horrible world, and so he made them marijuana cigarettes. For the Swedish reader of the novel, then, everybody in that military school smoked marijuana all the time.

I want to conclude by telling you a very funny anecdote, an anecdote which is like one of the episodes of the novel. After I left Peru in 1959, I had not heard a word about this Bolivian soap-opera writer. When I had finished the novel, but before it was printed, an Argentine journalist interviewed me and published an article in *La Nación* in which I told him about the novel and explained that it was based on a character I had met in Lima in the early fifties, a soap-opera writer who had some kind of psychic trouble. This character gave me the idea for writing the novel. I committed the grave error of naming this Bolivian. The article was published in Argentina; I was living in Spain at the time. One day I read in one of the Spanish newspapers a cable sent from La Paz, Bolivia, by this man who was an important person at that time in his country. He was mayor of La Paz and owned a chain of radio stations in Bolivia. He responded furiously to the article because apparently this interview, published in *La Nación* in Argentina, had been totally transformed by the Bolivian press into something very stupid because it said I was writing a novel about a Bolivian who went mad and was put away in a psychiatric clinic. The mayor of La Paz charged calumny and said he was going to sue Vargas Llosa and write a book about his activities in Bolivia, where he was well known for his links with the mafia and his homosexual deeds. Obviously, the Bolivian's imagination was still alive. When I published the novel, I sent him a copy with a kind letter in which I said he is not mentioned by name and should not be so angry. I have not seen him since then, but he is still very popular and still mayor of La Paz. He won the last election and now he is not so unhappy with the story because the fact that he was the source of inspiration for Pedro Camacho has apparently given him added popularity in Bolivia.

⋄ 7 ⋄

The Author's Favorite of His Novels
The War of the End of the World

If I had to choose one of my novels from among all I have published, I would probably choose *La Guerra del fin del mundo* (*The War of the End of the World*) because I think it is the most ambitious project I have ever undertaken. It is also the book on which I worked the longest and with the most difficulty. I say this for many reasons, but mostly for two. First, it was the first novel I wrote that is not located in my country, in Peru, but in a foreign country, Brazil. And second, this is also the first book that is not contemporary with my own life, but a historical book situated at the end of the nineteenth century. If you asked me fifteen years ago whether I would ever write a book with these characteristics—not situated in Peru and not contemporary— my answer would probably have been "No, never." I always write books about Peru and all of them have been contemporary.

In spite of the fact that I always thought my vocation was to write contemporary stories, always located among my people and among landscapes familiar to me, among people who speak my language, a language I could invent easily, one day I had an experience that was so powerful that it stimulated me to write about something else, to write *The War of the End of the World*. This experience was reading a book, an extraordinary book called

123

Os sertões by a Brazilian writer, Euclides da Cunha.[1] *Os sertões* is one of the most extraordinary books ever written in Latin America and an essential book for understanding what Latin America is or, better still, what Latin America is not. Anyone who wants to understand, to specialize in Latin American problems and cultures, should start by reading *Os sertões*.

I think *Os sertões* is one of the books I have read with the most amazement, enthusiasm, and passion. Why was I so impressed with this book? The reasons are many. First, at the time I read *Os sertões* some specific problems pertaining to Latin America were bothering me very much. One was: How is it possible for the intellectuals in Latin America—people of ideas, cultured people, people who are closely informed about what is going on in our countries, people who generally have traveled a great deal and for that reason can compare what happened in one country with what happened in another and can have a general outlook or perspective on Latin American problems— to have been responsible so many times for the conflicts and troubles Latin America has faced in its history? What is the reason that intellectuals have contributed, for instance, to intolerance, which is one of the darkest aspects of our history. Intellectuals have promoted intolerance, religious intolerance in the past and ideological and political intolerance in the present. It is true that intellectuals have also been victims of intolerance many times; they have been persecuted, sent to prison, tortured, sometimes killed by dictatorships. But in their political statements, they have reacted to this kind of intolerance in many, many cases with an

1. Euclides da Cunha (1866–1909). Civil engineer and journalist by profession, Cunha was also the author of four historical works, none of which has achieved the great acclaim that *Os sertões* (1902) has in Brazil and all Latin America. *Os sertões* describes a revolt against the newly established Republic of Brazil that took place in the "sertão," the remote backlands in the state of Bahia. Cunha served as a reporter covering the efforts of the federal troops to put down the rebellion.

equivalent intolerance, promoting a kind of zealous and dogmatic interpretation of our society and our reality. Why is this so? Why have the educated people of our continent participated in the same way as other sections of our society in the creation of this system of intolerance, which is at the root of our problems? Unfortunately, for many reasons intellectuals in Latin America are still ideologically oriented in their approach to political, social, and cultural problems. There are exceptions, of course; but in general I would say that, if the pragmatic approach is, as I think it is, more civilized and better able to understand what reality is, then the common people in Latin America probably have a clearer understanding of what is good for Latin America than do intellectuals and artists.

Reading *Os sertões* provided me with an extraordinary description of what this problem had been in one particular case, Brazil, and in one particular event, the civil war of Canudos. I was deeply moved by the case of Euclides da Cunha himself, the author of *Os sertões,* because his experience was like an incarnation of that of many intellectuals in the past and in the present in Latin America. Besides, I was greatly impressed because I think the book is a masterwork. It is not a novel, but it can be read as an extraordinary novel.[2]

The book is a description of something that happened in Brazil in the last years of the nineteenth century. I will summarize this civil war, this Canudos[3] war, because I assume that most North Americans have never heard of these episodes, as is also the case in Latin America. As you probably know, Brazilian independence came late in the nineteenth century, and it was in a comparatively pacific transition from the monarchy to the re-

2. A good English translation of *Os sertões,* by Samuel Putnam, entitled *Rebellion in the Backlands,* is still available.
3. Canudos. Antonio Conselheiro and his fanatic followers used an abandoned ranch called Canudos as their base of operations for the revolt. The term *Canudos* has come to refer to the revolt itself.

public. The republic was established in 1888 by a military coup that was supported in general by all westernized Brazil. The republican movement, which crushed the monarchy and replaced it, was a progressive movement in which the military and the intellectuals were the driving forces. The military and the intellectuals were united; it was one of the few occasions in Latin America when these two groups shared common political and social goals, a common purpose.

There was, for instance, a very interesting character, a military man and an intellectual named Benjamin Constant, who was a teacher at a military school in Rio de Janeiro. He had been deeply influenced by French positivist philosophy. He was an enthusiastic reader of French philosophy and thought that Auguste Comte was really the great thinker of the times. And so he introduced positivism in the military school in Rio de Janeiro, and many officers were educated in positivist ideas. As you have probably heard, positivism was very important in several Latin American countries, particularly in Brazil and Mexico. But the country where positivism was the most influential and where it became an official philosophy of the government and society was Brazil. In Brazil, positivism had much more influence than in France itself. I think that Brazil was the only place in the world where these temples of reason that Comte suggested were actually built, temples that should be oriented toward Paris as the mosques are oriented toward Mecca. In Brazil, some temples were built with this orientation. Benjamin Constant, in the military school in Rio de Janeiro, taught the young officers that the only way for Brazil to become a modern country, a progressive society, was to become a republic, substitute this old-fashioned, obsolete system of monarchy with a republic.

This was also the idea of all the progressive intellectuals of Brazil; and so when the military rebelled against the monarchy, the intellectuals supported them, and all civilized Brazil followed and accepted the republic. The republic was established in 1888 with great popular enthusiasm and with the conviction that it would transform Brazil into something similar to the United States of America. The United States was one of the models the Brazilians had in mind when they established the republic. They were people really convinced that the republic would change the lot of the poor people in Brazil, that the republic would mean not only modernization but also social justice, the disappearance or at least the diminution of all social and economic inequalities. They were progressive in the deepest sense of the word. It took some time of course for the republican institutions to be established all over this enormous country, to reach the remote areas of Brazil.

A few years after the republic was established, in a remote and isolated area in the interior of the state of Bahia, a place that had been developing or more or less languishing without communication with the rest of the country, there was a rebellion, a rebellion against the republic. And the rebels were probably the poorest people of Brazil. They were peasants, "cowboys," people who rebelled against the institution, against the republic. At the beginning, no one knew about this rebellion because the region was so isolated that only the authorities in Salvador, the capital of the state of Bahia, received information about it. And so they sent a company of the civil guard to crush this movement, a movement they considered very important. But the rebels defeated this company and took all the weapons. This unexpected outcome created some concern in Salvador, and this time a battalion was sent, led by Major Febronio DeBrito.

This second expedition was also defeated and destroyed by the rebels. Major DeBrito escaped, but all the weapons were taken by the rebels. This second defeat created an enormous scandal, this time all over the country. In Rio, in São Paulo, for instance, there were many meetings about the situation. The interesting thing was that nobody could understand what was going on because in the mind of the elite, the political, intellectual, military elite of the country, it was simply unthinkable that there was a rebellion of poor people against something that had been created precisely for their benefit, for the peasants, for the victims of Brazil. Westernized Brazilians could not understand the peasant's resistance, and they searched for an explanation.

It was at this moment that the progressive intellectuals of Brazil began to play a fundamental role. Because they could not understand what was happening, they did what all intellectuals do when they fail to understand something: they invented a theory. The theory was that this was not a rebellion of the poor peasants of the northeast, Bahia, which was unthinkable. This was a rebellion of the enemies of the republic. And who are the enemies of the republic? They are the monarchists, the old members of the court, the officers who are exiled in Buenos Aires or in Lisbon, and of course the landowners in the interior of Bahia, these rich people who are the natural enemies of the republic. The monarchists were the people really responsible for the rebellion. And England was also responsible because it was a natural enemy of the republic. The monarchy had had a close commercial and economic relationship with England. As the republic wanted to orient its trade more toward the United States of America, England suffered because of this policy. For this reason, the intellectuals thought that England intervened in the rebellion. The rebellion was in fact a conspiracy created by the enemies of the republic. What is really fascinating is that this theory, an imaginary creation of the politicians and intellectuals, of westernized Brazil, took shape little by little and became an incontrovertible reality, something so obvious that nobody thought of falsifying or criticizing it.

Euclides da Cunha, who was a fanatical republican, a man totally convinced of the necessity of the republic in order to modernize Brazil and create social justice in the country (he had been expelled from the military academy in Rio de Janeiro because he refused to salute a minister of the monarchy), was working at that time as a journalist in São Paulo and wrote vehement articles against the rebels in the northeast, calling this rebellion "our vendetta" because of the French reactionary movement in Britain against the French Revolution.

The republic sent a third military expedition to crush the rebellion and made Colonel Moreira César, a famous republican officer in Brazil, head of this expeditionary force. He had also been a fanatical republican and positivist and had been fighting for the republic ever since he was a young officer. He was a military star; great military deeds studded his career. He had crushed a small rebellion against the republic in Santa Catalina, an event in which he showed terrible cruelty. He was a hero to the republic, and his Seventh Regiment was one of the star branches of the army. Colonel César's regiment was sent to crush the rebellion, and, of course, the whole country was waiting for the result. The rebels also defeated Moreira César. They killed him and many of his lieutenants; they kept most of the weapons of the Seventh Regiment.

You can imagine how this news was received in Rio and other cities of Brazil. In Rio there were spontaneous demonstrations of the masses against the monarchists, who were still living there. Some of the monarchists were lynched by the protestors; some monarchists' journals, which were still being published, were burned. It was really a national scandal. In the newspapers, there were articles explaining how Moreira César was defeated because the British navy had directly participated in the rebellion with weapons, with explosive material that had been smuggled into the backlands of Bahia, and how British officers and monarchist officers were actually fighting with the rebels.

All of this was in the newspapers. There is a very interesting book written by a Brazilian sociologist called *Na calor da hora* (In the Heat of the Hour), which is a description of what the newspapers said about the rebellion. It is fascinating to read this book because you can see how journalism and history at a given moment can become a branch of fiction, exactly like poetry or the novel. After César's defeat, practically half of the Brazilian army was sent on a fourth expedition to fight the rebels. Euclides da Cunha went on this expedition and stayed a few weeks in Canudos, where the rebellion took place. He could see with his own eyes what was going on in this rebel citadel. It is a pedagogical experience to read what he wrote in the articles he sent to his São Paulo newspaper from the front. Although he was there and could see who the rebels were, in fact he was totally blind. He was an extremely honest intellectual who was so convinced of his ideas that he could see only what his ideology allowed him to see. And so in his articles he wrote about naval officers with fair hair and who were obviously English officers. He wrote about explosives that only the British army had and mentioned one episode that was widely commented on by the press at the time—a very important shipment of British weapons that had been discovered in Salvador.

Of course, the fourth expedition crushed the rebellion. All the rebels were killed; it was one of the most horrible massacres in Latin American history, and it was said that at least forty thousand people were killed by the Brazilian army. Canudos was totally destroyed because the rebels never surrendered—they were killed. After the massacre, the army decided to destroy all the houses that were still standing. It was like an unconscious will to have all traces of what had happened disappear. All the houses were destroyed and the survivors, a few women and children, were sent all over the country to different families.

Euclides da Cunha was one of the first Brazilians to understand that something very tragic had happened, that a terrible misunderstanding lay behind this social tragedy. He was one of the first Brazilians to ask himself: What have we done to these people? Where are these British officers? Where are these landowners? Where are these Brazilian monarchists? All these poor people are peasants, illiterate people who have no idea of what

Brazil is, people who fought the army shouting "Life to Jesus." And Cunha became extremely worried and anguished, with terrible feelings about what civilized Brazil had done to the rebels. He tried to understand what had really happened. How was it possible for a country like Brazil to have been submerged in this national confusion? Euclides da Cunha's book *Os sertões* is the explanation he gives himself, his country, and posterity of what Canudos was, how Canudos was possible, and how the civil war was possible.

It took him three years to write this book. It is said that it took him the same time to build a bridge. An engineer, he worked very far from Canudos building this bridge and did both things simultaneously. *Os sertões* is an extraordinary book because it is both a personal and a national self-criticism. By trying to understand what Canudos was, what this rebellion was, I think Cunha discovered what Latin America is, what a Latin American country is and, as I said before, what a Latin American country is not. What he showed in his book is that importing institutions, ideas, values, and even aesthetic tendencies from Europe to Latin America is something that can have very different consequences, something that can produce unexpected results. He explained the rebellion, for instance, as a deformation of religious ideas that were imported to Brazil and imposed on this community of peasants. These people were educated by fanatical Catholic *integristas,* monks who preached a kind of intolerance and dogmatic vision that was profoundly assimilated by this isolated community of the *caboclos* in the interior of Bahia, people who found in this religion the only source of relief from their terrible sufferings.

In this atmosphere many foolish deviations from established religions were possible. There were many preachers crossing the *sertões,* transforming religion into a kind of fanatical cult. One of these preachers was the leader of the rebellion, Antonio Conselheiro, a mysterious man with a mysterious youth and childhood, a man who had never been a politician before learning that the republic was established. When he found out, he immediately reacted not only as a religious leader but also as a politician, declaring that the republic was the antichrist. This is something he had learned from the missionaries, the Capuchin missionaries who had always preached against the idea of a republic, as something invented by the enemies of the church, by the Masons, for instance.

Antonio Conselheiro was a very coherent man, and when the republic was founded he reacted in a coherent way, with the doctrines and religious ideas he had always lived by. He thought that because the antichrist was already in Brazil, the people must be prepared to fight against him. As Christians that was their obligation. That was the driving force behind the rebellion, the religious idea that evil was in Brazil and that the Christians, the authentic Christians, should fight against this scourge. What is extraordinary is that the people followed Conselheiro and accepted his ideas. They followed because they could understand what Conselheiro was telling them. Conselheiro was a charismatic figure; he had a way of reaching the minds and hearts of very simple people like the peasants. On the other hand they could not understand the positivist ideas that were behind the republic, this abstract institution of the republic, these representative bodies. All such abstractions were totally remote from their daily lives. It was, however, easy for them to transform these abstract notions into something suspect, into something that could be incarnate danger for their lives and even more for their souls. When these foreigners arrived (and these military troops were foreigners, for the peasants had never seen people from Rio or São Paulo), they felt their culture was threatened. They had a culture of their own, a culture made up of primitive things, primitive customs, dogmatic religious ideas, but a culture that gave them a feeling of belonging to something that was shared by all of them. They had nothing to share with these foreigners, who arrived there with Moreira César talking about the republic and positivist ideas. These foreigners were even atheists, like César, who considered religion an obstacle to progress and modernization. For these peasants his beliefs confirmed that the republic was the antichrist. The whole society of Brazil was divided by reciprocal prejudices, by reciprocal intolerances, religious on the one side, ideological on the other. All these things produced the catastrophe.

For me all of this was like seeing in a small laboratory the pattern of something that had been happening all over Latin America since the beginning of our independence. All Latin American countries have had more or less similar situations. The division of society according to these reciprocal, dogmatic visions of what society should be, of what the political organization of society should be, had always had similar consequences—wars, repression, massacres. I was deeply moved by all Cunha described in *Os sertões* and immediately felt the need to fantasize about it and write a novel using Canudos—well, I would not say as a pretext because I was fascinated by Canudos, by the event itself that was such an extraordinary adventure. But at the same time I felt that if I wrote a persuasive novel using Canudos as a setting for that story, I would perhaps be able to present in fiction the description of a continental phenomenon, something that every Latin American could recognize as part of his own past and in some cases his own present because in contemporary Latin America you still have Canudos in many countries. In Peru, for instance, we have a living Canudos in the Andes.

I therefore decided to use the historical events of Canudos as the raw material to write a novel in which I would be totally free to change, deform, and invent situations, using the historical background only as a point of departure to create what essentially would be a fiction, that is, a literary invention. I decided to follow the general historical episodes, the four military expeditions, and to use some of the historical figures, such as Colonel Moreira César or Conselheiro, the leader of the rebels, as literary figures, but without respecting their biographies and freely adopting what I felt was useful for my literary purposes. I believe I have read everything that has been written about Canudos. I was fascinated during the investigation because I was constantly discovering that the material was particularly rich and suggestive for fiction. The entire republican history of the war was well documented. The rebel side was not documented at all. There were no documents written by the rebels. Some of the survivors among the rebels had been interviewed, but very late in their lives. There was, for instance, some written material on Villanova, one of the leaders of the rebellion, who was found by a journalist when he was an old man and interviewed. A document was produced, one of the few from the rebels.

All this gave me a great opportunity to invent, to fantasize about what happened to the rebels, what happened in the Canudos citadel. I remember how moved I was one day when I discovered while reading, although I do not recall what book or article in a newspaper, that someone said that among the rebels in the citadel there was a kind of monster, a very deformed individual from Natuba who knew how to write. The idea that among the rebels there was at least one person who knew how to write and who had probably written something there was for me extremely moving. I was deeply touched by the idea that there may be a potential writer among the rebels.

From this discovery I created a whole character, a very important character in my novel called León de Natuba, who is a writer, someone who is very close to Conselheiro, writing down everything he says, documenting what is happening there. I used the names of some of Conselheiro's lieutenants, but I invented their biographies. One exciting aspect of the rebellion was that once the war started everybody in the region reached the citadel, the rebel site. Some village priests went there to fight with Conselheiro, who was considered a heretic by the official judge.

But in spite of that the village priests in the region had formed a natural solidarity with these persons. And so they fought alongside the rebels. All the criminals of the region (the *cangaceiros,* although the name was not popular at that time), these gangs of bandits, immediately joined the rebel citadel and were really the military chiefs of the rebellion.

Pajeú was a very famous bandit in the region who became Conselheiro's right hand. In Pajeú's biography I used what could be called a stereotypical pattern of what a bandit was in the *sertão* at that time. I decided to write first a version of the novel without visiting the region, without looking with my eyes at the *sertão,* at the places where the rebellion happened. And that is what I did. I worked two years on a very long first version of the novel. It was only when I had finished this version that I went to Bahia, to Salvador, and to the *sertão.* I was lucky enough to be accompanied in this journey by a Brazilian, an anthropologist named Renato Ferash, who had been director of the Museum of Modern Art in Salvador; who knew the *sertão* very well and the *caboclos* (people of the region); who was familiar with the history and sociology of the area; and who had many friends in the villages in the *sertão.*

Ferash's acceptance was really a great help to me because the *caboclos* are reserved, very different from the people of the coastal area of Bahia, in Salvador, who are extroverted. The *caboclo* is a closed society that distrusts foreigners. But Renato Ferash was considered one of them, and they were completely receptive to him. We went to visit the twenty-five small villages in the *sertão* where it is said Conselheiro preached. We even saw the village where the church built by Conselheiro himself still stands. For the people in the region, Canudos, the civil war, was still present and very much alive because it was the most important and perhaps the only important event in their lives. All families there had some parent or grandparent who had been in the rebellion, and everybody had heard anecdotes and episodes of the war. The songs that had been sung at the time were still sung by the people, and we heard many of these war songs. All this, as you can imagine, was extremely rich as material for the novel.

I was impressed when I discovered that the reason for the war was also still very much alive. I remember how in some places the questions I asked about Canudos provoked terrible discussions among people. There were people who justified the intervention, explaining that that was the only way in which Brazil could become a modern and integrated society, that the rebels were cruel people. It was sad, no doubt, but what can a republic, what can a modern state do when there is a rebellion of primitive people who fight society's institutions, that consider institutions the antichrist? Can the republic surrender to this kind of fanaticism? Its obligation was to defend law and order, and that was the reason it crushed Canudos.

On the other hand I remembered that Father Gumercindo, a small village priest, vehemently defended these rebels, explaining that the corruption of the contemporary church resulted in people like the republicans winning that war, that the history of the church would have been very different if people like Conselheiro had won the war. He explained that Conselheiro was the real church, a church not corrupted by modern ideas. It was amazing to see how all the problems that had been behind Canudos were still there in the region.

Of course, the most important moment in this journey was when I arrived at Canudos itself. Canudos does not exist any more; it is now an artificial lake. A dam was created. The place where the citadel was located is now submerged under the water, and the people in the region say, "You see, Conselheiro was right because he announced that the *sertão tornaria mar* (the desert would become a sea). Of course, the water is there, and so he was correct. Still to be seen on the shores of the lake was the cross that people said was once on the tower of the church of Canudos and the whole area is still full of cartridges from the war. After this visit, I rewrote the novel two more times, and only after the last version did I feel myself more secure, or less insecure, than when I had written the first draft. As I have mentioned, I never had such enormous difficulty writing a novel, but at the same time I was never so excited with the subject as with *The War of the End of the World,* and this, of course, helped me overcome all my problems.

One of my major difficulties was to figure out in what language these people should speak because I write in Spanish and they speak Portuguese. And because I write all my novels in a realistic way, I had to determine what kind of language they were going to use, a language that would not sound artificial to the reader. I tried to create a language that is not entirely Spanish in spite of being Spanish, a language in which some *lusitanismos,* some Portuguese words, would be introduced in order to give Brazilian color to the phrases, to the language. I used this not only in the dialogue but also in the descriptions.[4] I had the idea of giving the novel the structure of a novel of adventure. Because I had always been a great admirer of literature of adventure, Canudos was an extraordinary occasion for me to write an epic novel of adventure, with many anecdotes and episodes, a novel in which military events would be important. I have received many literary influences from both historical and literary works. One of the things that was a great surprise to me as I traveled in Bahia was to discover that this chivalrous tradition was still alive in that part of Brazil, in the form of the "literatura de cordel" (epic literature), which reached Brazil with the Portuguese. It has now totally vanished in Portugal, but in the *sertão* you can hear chivalrous songs recited by the troubadours.

4. Incidentally, Helen Lane, who translated *The War of the End of the World* into English, knows both Spanish and Portuguese very well, and she is also very familiar with Euclides da Cunha and with the historical events that serve as raw material for the book. She worked carefully, and I think it is a good translation. It may be better than the original.

I immediately used these songs in my novel as homage to the tradition of chivalry and also because it is something that remains in the contemporary culture of the *sertão*. The novel would also be a novel of great spaces, a novel that would move the story with great freedom. I thought it important that the structure and form of the novel should also help give the contemporary reader the necessary distance he has vis-à-vis the events that took place almost a century ago. In some episodes of the novel I deliberately used a kind of phrase, a kind of writing that would give a flavor, a reminiscence of nineteenth-century narrative. I decided that some people and some events in the novel should be presented to the reader at a great distance, that it was important, for instance, that Conselheiro should be perceived by the reader as he had been perceived by his followers, not as a human, flesh-and-blood figure, but as a mythical figure, as a divine kind of presence. For that reason it was important for Conselheiro to be far away from the reader at all times. The narrator never approaches Conselheiro; he is always looking at him from the perspective of his followers and describing him as he is perceived and felt by people who believe him to be a kind of divine incarnation. I narrated all these episodes in a nineteenth-century style, but I alternated them with episodes that had a modern approach.

Many years before I read Euclides da Cunha, I had the idea of writing a novel or short story, a piece of fiction, about a character I had imagined while reading a history of Spanish anarchism. You know that anarchism was very important in Spain in the nineteenth century; in some regions anarchism became a popular movement. In Andalucía and in Cataluña, for instance, anarchism was really popular. While reading a history of anarchism, I found that a group of anarchists in Barcelona had been especially impressed with phrenology (this pseudoscience created by a man named Franz Joseph Gall), according to which the bones of the head were considered the materialization of the soul, of the moral and psychological characteristics of an individual. An expert phrenologist, by touching the bones of someone's head, could immediately determine his characteristics. Those Catalan anarchists were very impressed with Gall's ideas and decided that phrenology was the scientific convention for materialism, that in phrenology the basic justification for philosophical materialism was confirmed. Thus they became anarchist phrenologists, or phrenological anarchists.

I was excited when I read the ideas of these anarchist phrenologists or phrenological anarchists. They really thrilled me, and I decided to write a novel or a short story with an anarchist phrenologist as a character. But it was difficult because I was writing novels about contempory Peru. How could I put a phrenologist there? It was alien to my usual themes. When I started writing *The War of the End of the World,* however, my anarchist phrenologist was immediately in a familiar setting. So I put my phrenologist/anarchist in Canudos, in this novel of reciprocal fanaticisms. This gave the novel an added dimension—the foreigner who comes to Latin America in order to find his personal visions, his utopia. This is an important aspect of our history, foreigners who come to Latin America and see not what Latin America is but what they would like Latin America to be so that they may satisfy their personal visions. We have a long list of people of this kind, starting with Columbus, of course. He wanted to reach India; he stumbled on Latin America and saw India.

I wanted this phrenologist/anarchist to incarnate in the novel this very authentic character of the foreigner who is as misguided about our reality as Conselheiro is for religious reasons or as Colonel Moreira César is for philosophical reasons. In his case it is utopia that blinds him about the reality that surrounds him. He became one of the main characters of the novel. I wanted Euclides da Cunha to be there also; I wanted someone who could incarnate what he personified better than anyone else during this war. This Latin American intellectual—clever, intelligent, cultured, well-intentioned about our realities—is, in spite of all that, so ideologically oriented that he can become an essential factor in our tragedies, in our political catastrophes. I used the case of Euclides da Cunha to create a character in the novel who is a journalist. He is the only character who is never named in the novel. He is a shortsighted journalist (that is the only way he is described in The War of the End of the World), who is just one of the witnesses of the story, a story that he cannot really understand when living through the episode, but who afterwards makes a great effort to understand the situation and writes the book that would provide the real explanation of what happened in Canudos.

I wanted literature, the written word, to be an important character in the novel, too, because when I was doing research for Canudos I discovered that the written word was an essential figure in what happened. It was because the newspapers said certain things about Canudos, because speeches were made and then published, because lectures were given about what was happening, that all this national misunderstanding was possible. And so this written word, a word that was supposed to describe and interpret reality, was in fact transforming and changing it, as fiction frequently does. The written word was witness to the tragedy of Canudos. I wanted literature to be there, to be present as a real character, manipulating events and pushing people to assume definite attitudes. This aspect—the written word—is very important in the novel. There are articles in newspapers that appear in the novel, for instance, describing political discussions in an assembly. Also included are letters exchanged among the characters that describe events and cause people to change their actions and attitudes toward Canudos.

I had great difficulty in inventing a convincing dialogue for the peasants, the "cowboys," the poorest people in The War of the End of the World. In the novel, these people usually do not speak directly to the reader. What they say, their words, are usually filtered through intermediaries, people from the middle class—intellectuals, physicians, journalists, landowners—whose language was for me more easily brought out and invented. This helped to create a society in the novel that is as much divided as it actually was in Brazil during the war. The narrator exposes the reader much more to the civilized, German Brazil, westernized Brazil; and through literary devices he keeps a certain distance from the other side of the country. This imbalance gives the language of the novel the personality of a divided world in which there are two societies totally unable to communicate with each other. Thus the main concern of *The War of the End of the World* is not the religious or political differences that exist in Brazil and, by extension, throughout Latin America, but the divisiveness of these two societies caused by their inability to communicate.

› 8 ‹

Transforming a Lie into Truth
The Real Life of Alejandro Mayta as a Metaphor for the Writer's Task

Historia de Mayta is a novel that has been given the English title of *The Real Life of Alejandro Mayta*. I must say that I do not like the translation of the title because in Spanish *historia* means both history and story. My translator and my publisher told me that it was impossible to have one word for both ideas as we have in Spanish, and so it would be better to change the title to *The Real Life of Alejandro Mayta,* which is a bit misleading because the novel is not about the "real" life of Alejandro Mayta, but just the opposite, the fictitious, the imaginary life of Alejandro Mayta. I had a strange experience with this novel. I am aware that a writer does not have the last word about what he has written. I know that in many cases a critic or reader can have a better picture or understanding of what a writer has done in a novel or poem. Only in this case, in this book, I had the feeling of having written a novel perceived by the critics and readers as something very different from what I thought. My goals, my motivations in this book were not what readers imagined. And I am not saying that critics and readers were wrong; what I am saying is that maybe my deliberate planning of this book, my conscious work when I was writing it, was less important than my unconscious feeling, my unconscious intervention. Anyway, you can judge for yourselves.

What I shall try to do now is tell you what kind of book I wanted to write. You will see if this is something that matches the real book or not. *Historia de Mayta* has been read mostly as a political book and in many cases has been considered a political essay about violence, revolution, upheavals, social unrest, and turmoil in Latin America; a political statement disguised as a novel, presented in the form of a novel, a book in which what is essential is the description of an objective and historical reality. That, of course, was not my intention when I wrote it. I knew I was using political matters, ideology, some historical facts and events as raw material in this novel; but my goal was literary, not political. As I mentioned earlier, if you want to make a political statement, it is much better to write an essay or article or deliver a lecture than to use a genre like the novel, which was created not to convey objective statements but instead to present an illusory feeling of reality. The novel should create an illusion of reality rather than present an objective and specific knowledge of what reality is in any field. Although I do not disregard political readings of novels, their value depends upon the critic. There are intelligent and creative critics who, while they are artificial and arbitrary in their judgment and use politics as a perspective to write about literature, can offer something original and persuasive even if they disagree with the conclusions of the work. Because a novel is an illusion of a living experience, it can be approached from different perspectives—political, religious, moral, sociological, and linguistic.

As in the case of all my books, *Historia de Mayta* also started as a personal experience, not an experience that I lived myself but something I knew extremely well. Again, as I have said, during the late fifties and early sixties I was politically committed to extreme leftist causes and ideals. Like many Latin Americans, my enthusiasm for the triumph of the Cuban revolution was very strong. When Fidel Castro entered Havana, that was something extremely important for the Left in Latin America. At that time I was part of the Left in spite of the fact that I had broken with the Communist party of which I had been a member for one year. I had been very close to leftist ideals; the idea of socialism was extremely appealing to me. I was very enthusiastic about Marxism in general in spite of having many doubts and disagreements with some aspects of Marxism, particularly the Marxist approach to aesthetics, to literature, to art. But the triumph of the Cuban revolution meant a great deal to people like me because for the first time we thought that revolution was something possible in our countries. Until then the idea of revolution was romantic and remote to us, something we took more as an academic idea that could never become a reality in countries like ours.

What happened in Cuba changed this attitude. It showed that revolution was possible, that a Latin American country could become a Socialist country. While giving us this example, Cuba also gave us a method by which to bring this ideal into being. Che Guevara's conclusion about the Cuban revolution, that the objective conditions for a revolution could be created by revolutionaries, was something that I think psychologically changed the attitude of the extreme Left in Latin America. Like many Latin Americans, I was deeply moved and excited with what was happening in Cuba. But I was nonetheless amazed when one day I read in *Le Monde* (I was living in France at the time) that a group of Peruvians had actually attempted to start a revolution in the central Andes. They had taken control of the small city of Jauja for a few hours and then escaped to the mountains. They were hunted down; some were killed, and others arrested by the civil guards.

Until I read this report, I had never really believed that in Peru, in a country like mine, in a country I thought I knew so well, this would happen one day. I was impressed, and the idea that this group of people had attempted a revolution and been defeated, that they had dared to do something so many people in Peru had been thinking about without having the drive to carry it out, was something I kept in my memory. As in other incentives for writing, it gradually became a matter for literary speculation, something around which both my imagination and my fantasy started to work and build.

Sometime later, just by chance, I met a man in France who knew the details of what had happened and how this attempt had been prepared and organized, all of which I found interesting. It seems that this revolutionary attempt was something quite crazy because the revolutionaries consisted of only two adults and a group of students from a high school in Juaja; they were just a handful of people, I do not remember how many, maybe ten or fifteen. They were not twenty in any case. It was difficult to imagine how this group of people might be able to start a revolution and a process by which it could control the country.

One of the leaders, one of the two adults, was a young lieutenant of the Guardia Republicana, which is one branch of the army, who was only twenty-two or twenty-three years old. The other leader was a man in his early forties named Mayta, the only one who had a political background, a political militancy. First he had been in the Communist party, in the Soviet section of the Communist party; then he was a Maoist, the other faction of the Communists in Peru. After being expelled from the Maoist group, he became a Trotskyite. He was a militant of a very small Trotskyite group when he met this young lieutenant by accident, who to his amazement started to talk about the possibilities of a revolution in Peru. The lieutenant had no kind of ideological education. He was a spontaneous revolutionary, but this Trotskyite was impressed when he heard that this enthusiast for revolution was a militant.

In Peru, as in many other Latin American countries at that time, it was unthinkable to associate a military man, an officer, with revolution, with Marxism. Not now, but thirty years ago a young officer was exactly the opposite of a revolutionary. Things have changed considerably since then, and now there are military men who are sympathetic to leftist causes, just as there are priests today who are sympathetic to extreme leftist doctrines, which was also rare at that time. It was decided in this Trotskyite group that Mayta should try to indoctrinate this officer in order to enlist him in the group. Mayta tried to indoctrinate him politically. At the beginning the idea of revolution was apparently something important for Mayta from an ideological point of view, something impractical, something not possible in a country like Peru.

However, during the friendship that was established between these two men, it was in fact the young officer who indoctrinated and convinced the trained revolutionary Mayta that the revolution was actually possible, that Peru was a fertile land for an upheaval. He explained to Mayta that he was based in Jauja and that the town could be easily captured by a group of revolutionaries, that they could get all the weapons from the city guard there, and that they could establish a revolutionary focal point in the mountains, in the Andes. That was one of the strategic innovations of the Cuban revolution, that the revolution could establish a focus, which, if it managed to survive, would little by little infect the masses, the peasants, the victims of society. This revolutionary focus would increase through violent action.

The Troskyite was convinced and accepted, and so together they planned the revolution. At first, many people agreed to participate. Then when the deadline was reached, they became skeptical about the plan and withdrew. The only ones left were these two men and a group of students who according to the original plan were supposed to have only a marginal role as messengers in the revolution, but who at the last moment were incorporated fully into the scheme. That is the story behind the event I found out about in the French newspaper.

That story gave me the initial idea for *Historia de Mayta.*
I wanted to write something about that event, and I think at that
time, in 1962, what I had in mind was a political novel of adventure—to tell a story in which a handful of people are crazy
enough or generous enough or idealistic enough to attempt a
revolution. This would be a very small adventure lasting just a
few hours, as in the original pact. But it would be presented in
my book as an adventure story. That, again, was my first idea.
I never start writing immediately after I have an idea. My usual
pace is to think about it for months and years and to enrich the
original idea. Then one day I start taking notes and putting these
anecdotes into place. But this original plan, this original image
for the novel changed with my own political evolution. In the
sixties, my enthusiasm for the revolution slowly diminished; that
is, my belief in the method of violent action against the status
quo and the establishment, the idea that only violence could really
break the status quo and precipitate economic and social reform
in our country. My conviction altered, and I was disappointed
at what Cuba had become and what real socialism was when
you visited the Socialist countries.

At the same time, in Peru and all over Latin America, this
revolutionary idea was growing, gaining more and more people,
particularly those from the middle class, but also some workers
and peasants. It took deep roots mostly at the university level
of society, among middle-class intellectuals and the political avant-
garde. During the sixties there were many attempts in Peru and
elsewhere to establish military focal points in the mountains. Some
friends of mine were involved in this activity. Several people who
had been living in Paris when I was there went to participate
in guerrilla action in Peru in the mid-sixties. Many of them were
killed there, others were put in prison. I could follow quite closely
what was happening with this idea of revolution in Peru; and
all this material was incorporated, consciously or unconsciously,
into my original idea of a novel about revolution in my country.

I think this melding of thoughts also changed the plan, the project, of the novel.

In the early seventies another idea, probably more important than the original idea of a novel of political adventure, took over. It was an idea related to fiction. Ever since I wrote *Captain Pantoja and the Special Service,* but mostly after writing *Aunt Julia and the Scriptwriter,* fiction as a subject, as a theme, was something that became very interesting and very important to me. Fiction as something larger than literature, fiction as something much more important in life than literature or art. I discovered that in fact fiction is indispensable for mankind, even for people who have never read a book or who are not interested in literature. I do not think there are too many people who can do without fiction; everyone needs to incorporate into his real life a fictitious life, some kind of lie that by some mechanism or other he transforms into truth. In many cases literature accomplishes this task. We read novels, we are thrilled, we are enriched by this fictitious lie that the novel gives us when we are reading it. This is a very conscious way of incorporating a fiction into our lives. But there are many other ways in which it is not so clear that we are incorporating this fictitious dimension into our own experience. In many cases religion accomplishes this function for a person or for a society.

I recognized this human need for the fictitious experience even more when I became involved in political debates in Latin America, when I started to change my vision of social problems, when I became more and more critical of extreme Left strategies and ideas. I was deeply involved in polemics, and so I had to think a great deal about this subject. One day I reached this conclusion: that ideology in Latin America was fulfilling this task for many people; that ideology was the way they incorporated fiction into their lives, as other people incorporated the fictitious experience through fiction, through novels, or through religious ideas. Many young people, many intellectuals, many avant-garde politicians were using ideology, were using these political ideas that presumed to describe reality, to identify the laws of history and the mechanisms of society, evolution, and progress, and were, in fact, adding to reality a purely imaginary world.

It seemed very strange to me that this fiction, which took the name of political ideology, was a major source of violence and brutality in Latin America; that these sometimes elaborate and complex ideological constructions in which one society was described and then another ideal society was also described as a goal to be reached through revolution, as well as a methodology of the way this revolution could be achieved, were, in fact, a mechanism that was destroying our societies and creating major obstacles to real progress and the battle against the things the revolution opposes — social injustice, economic inequalities, lack of integration of the different cultures.

I thought it was interesting how fiction could have these two bases. In one way fiction can be beneficial for mankind. The great literary achievements in our history, in our civilization, have not only enriched mankind psychologically but also ethically; and they have encouraged progress in many ways. At the same time fiction has been a major instrument of suffering in history because it was behind all the dogmatic doctrines that have justified repression, censorship, massacres, and genocides. Why not, therefore, write a novel about these two faces, this reverse and obverse that fiction has? When I decided to do that, the story of Mayta, the story of this handful of revolutionaries, immediately came to mind. It was, in fact, ideal raw material for the invention of a novel in which this problem, these two faces, the night-and-day story of fiction, would materialize and be developed.

And so that is the novel that I thought I wrote. It is a novel, of course, in which there is a revolution, this revolutionary attempt by Mayta and his group of students and these young officers. I had some information about what had happened, but I started immediately to do some research. I did so not in order to be totally faithful to what had occurred, for I do not think that is the responsibility of a novelist. When you write a novel you do not have the obligation to be true and exact; the only obligation you have is to be persuasive. And to be persuasive as a novelist in most cases you are obliged to transform, to distort reality, to lie, to invent something that is not true—that is the only way fiction can be persuasive. I did so not to be objective, exact, truthful to reality, but, as the narrator of Mayta's story says: "Para mentir con conocimiento de causa." I do not like the translation of this phrase into English as it appears in the novel. What it really means is that one lies or distorts knowing that one is distorting.

I did a great deal of research. I went to the newspapers and magazines of that year. I read everything that had been written and tried to interview the participants, the people who had been involved in the affair. It was very interesting because the interviews helped me considerably in writing my novel. I discovered that although this revolutionary attempt had taken place twenty or twenty-five years ago, many people were extremely reluctant to say exactly what they knew. I discovered how they used their memories to justify what they had done, sometimes to take revenge on adversaries, and how in some cases the witnesses did this deliberately. It is obvious that they were lying in order to change the past. And in other cases, no; it was obvious they were unconsciously changing the past to justify the present, to justify what they were, to justify their evolution. Their statements were extremely interesting because I could test in a practical way how fiction was operating there. Fiction was something so visible— what they told me, what they said they remembered, what happened. For a writer, unlike an anthropologist or a historian, lies are as important as truth; they are equally useful. The important thing is the mechanism. That is the superiority of a fiction writer over a scholar.

I used all this in the novel to introduce different levels of description. My idea was that the novel would flow on two different levels: an objective level in which a narrator, someone who would have my name but only to misguide the reader once again, would try to collect material to write a novel about what had happened and how it had happened in this attempt. This would be the so-called fake objective level of the novel. There for the reader would be a writer in the process of collecting raw material, nourishment for his fantasy, for his imagination. There would be another level, an imaginary level, in which the reader would follow the process of building a fiction. The reader would see this writer using what he knows, what he reads, what he hears, what he discovers in objective reality as material out of which his fantasy and imagination construct a fiction, something that is not a reflection, not a totally separate reality (because this new reality is using this material all the time), but something that little by little becomes very different or rather essentially different from what the objective source of the fiction is. So the whole novel would be a continuous confrontation between these two dimensions, or faces, of one process that would have as protagonist the writer himself, the mind of the writer.

When I began working on *Historia de Mayta,* my idea was that the narrator would be an invisible character, just an instrument, a literary device to establish these two separate levels of the narration. But it happened differently. Little by little the narrator took on a clearer shape, became more important, became a real protagonist. Perhaps the narrator managed to become the protagonist of the novel. He is at least as important as Mayta because he is manipulating what happens in such a way that what is important at the end is not what happened but the way in which reality and the characters and the events are manipulated by this elusive personality that is the narrator. But this is something that occurred in the novel in an unconscious more than a deliberate way.

That is what the story of Mayta is, a novel about fiction, about two kinds of fiction, ideological fiction and literary fiction. Ideological fiction is what Mayta and his comrades live. Mayta is an ideologue, a man totally convinced that reality can be captured by the mechanisms of reason, by the mechanisms of a doctrine that is Marxism enriched and improved by Lenin and Trotsky, that provides all the instruments to understand exactly what society is, what forces are involved in history and how, knowing this, a revolutionary can act and produce qualitative changes in reality. The reader can perceive in the novel how this ideology is, in fact, a fiction—something that is constantly rejected or falsified by objective reality—but how in spite of that, Mayta has a mechanism that is immediately put into action whenever this falsification of reality and ideas occurs; and how the ideology immediately adapts itself to the new situation and finds a theoretical justification to move forward in the same illusory way. And the reader will perceive how all this leads Mayta and his followers into something that produces exactly the opposite result and consequences from what they expect.

On the other hand *Historia de Mayta* is a description of the other kind of fiction, a fiction that the narrator/writer is trying to write. The reader sees in the novel how this other fiction, which is also an imaginary construction that has some roots in reality, as in the case of this ideological fiction built by Mayta, does not have these negative or even catastrophic results but has positive ones because at least in this world, which is going to pieces, which is practically disappearing in an orgy of violence, this man who is writing finds a reason to resist, to live. He tells one of the witnesses when asked how he can stupidly write a novel at this time when the country is disappearing, when there is civil war and terrorism and people are dying from hunger: "No, it's not stupid. At least to write a novel is something that can create a way in which I can defend myself against all this catastrophe that surrounds me."

At least fantasy and imagination can psychologically provide a way to survive in spite of the fact that in objective reality there is no longer any hope. My idea was that through the destiny of the characters in a novel or short story I can make evident something I believe, that fiction is negative, has negative results for society and for history when it is not perceived as fiction, when it is disguised as objective knowledge, when it is an objective description of what reality is; and that on the contrary, fiction is positive and useful to society and history and the individual when it is perceived as fiction, when, while reading a novel or poem, you know that this idea of experiencing something real is an illusion, when you are not lying to yourself believing that this is not an illusion, but a factual experience. I would like the novel to make this paradox evident, that when fiction is perceived as fiction and accepted as such, it becomes part of reality and is transformed into something that is objective and factual reality. I think in this sense we incorporate novels into our lives because we are aware that novels are in fact not reality.

This fiction that is accepted as fiction, accepted as an illusion, can very easily be incorporated into our real experiences and give us a better understanding of ourselves and of what society is. On the other hand, fiction considered as objective science, as in the case of this ideology that compels Mayta and his comrades to act as they do, is something that precipitates in reality a very destructive process because it misguides people about what reality is and sometimes establishes a gap between the mind, the ideas, and the possibility to make effective changes.

That is the novel I wanted to write, and that is the novel I thought I had written when I finished the book. But this idea I had of the novel has not been brought out in any of the reviews, essays, or even oral commentaries I heard about the work. *Historia de Mayta,* as I said, has been taken as a political novel against revolution, a novel that is a kind of indictment of Marxism and revolutionary acts in Latin America. I do not know. I do not think a writer has the last word. In any case, it is interesting for some readers to know a writer's intention, a writer's goal when he wrote his book.

I do not think you can establish any kind of moral norm for a writer because you will always find more exceptions than confirmations. For some writers, to be a militant can be destructive; for others, it can be a great source of inspiration. Each writer is a specific case, and you cannot really establish one common denominator for what writing is, for what the best moral attitude in a writer is. A writer is someone who writes out of his experiences, and the experiences of one writer can be completely different from those of another. In *Historia de Mayta* I used all of my experiences as a writer of fiction, and the book stands as a metaphor for my vocation as a writer. The story of Mayta, then, is my own story of a writer writing his fiction. What the narrator does with Mayta is what I do each time I write a novel.

I will tell you an interesting anecdote that occurred when I was writing the novel. Something happened to me that gave me an idea, a new idea for the novel, an idea that was incorporated into the book. Even after finishing the novel, I was still unable to discover what had happened to the Trotskyite who was the leader of the rebellion. Nobody knew about him; he had really disappeared. All the revolutionaries in Lima, people who had known him, who had been his friends or his adversaries, had lost track of him. So I thought he was dead, that maybe he had gone abroad and was living in exile. No one knew a word. It was only when I was finishing the last version of the novel that someone called and told me that apparently he was in prison, that he had been in a prison in Lima for the past few years. And so I asked permission to visit him. When I received permission to enter the prison, he was no longer there. He had been released just a few days or weeks before.

Through a prison friend, I learned he was working in an

ice-cream parlor. I immediately went to see him. There he was, attending customers. I was so impressed because after writing about him for so long, I had begun to consider him as one of my characters, the materialization of something I had invented. I told him I had been writing a book about him for the past three years. Well, maybe he thought I was crazy or did not understand at the beginning what I was saying. I explained what my project was, and he told me "All right, I'll give you one night but no more."

We had a long conversation and I discovered I knew much more than he did about the revolution and many more details. When I showed him copies of newspapers and magazines, he was very impressed because he had never seen many of these articles. He had forgotten many things, but what was most impressive to me was to discover that in his life this was just an episode, just an event that had been diminished by other experiences much more important because they were probably more tragic. After his imprisonment for the Jauja revolution, he had been involved in other violent acts, some political, some criminal. In any case he had spent the last ten years in prison. He was not interested in politics any more. He was a frustrated man who despised politics, and any kind of committed action he immediately rejected. In this long conversation, the only moment in which he appeared to become moved and talk with some commitment was when he explained how in prison he and a friend established a shop to sell fruit juices and coffee and tea. He was very proud of that. His plan would completely change the system because he always gave very clean fruit to the customers. It was really very funny because that was the only moment in the conversation in which he seemed proud of something.

That gave me the idea for the last chapter of the novel. If you have read *Historia de Mayta,* you know that in the last chapter the narrator discovers that Mayta is alive. In a long conversation with Mayta, the narrator learns that Mayta has forgotten most of the story, that he is a totally different man from the Mayta the narrator has invented, from the Mayta he has been researching. The historical Mayta is one person, the Mayta he has been writing about is another person, and the real Mayta is still another person, a third person, someone who appears only in the last chapter of the novel as the extreme confirmation of the presence of fiction in the world in which this narrator has been operating.

It was in fact this conversation that gave me the idea for the last chapter, which I think is very important; for in a way it completely changes the idea that the reader has of the story. In this chapter, the reader should have the feeling that he is now totally cut off from objective reality, that the novel has been pushing him little by little toward an imaginary world. Until the last chapter he is unaware of this transition; in the last chapter there is no way to avoid knowing it. After the conversation there is no way for either the reader or the writer himself to differentiate between the real event and fiction because all the boundaries have vanished once the writer has introduced the real man into the novel. With his testimony, the real man changes everything previously described in the book, not only the fictitious level of reality but also whatever the reader thought was objective reality in the novel — even the vast documentation that also becomes fiction, also an invention.

I was very happy with this chapter. It gave me something that explicitly confirmed the literary nature of the book as something much more important than all the political elements that appear in the work. But in spite of this last chapter, critics and readers have perceived the novel in a different way.

My latest book, *In Praise of the Stepmother,* is a kind of experiment, something that was proposed to a painter and me by a publisher. The idea was that a painter and a writer should produce a book simultaneously, each one using the material provided by the other. I would write a synopsis of a story, and the painter would use it to draw something. I then would use this drawing as a source for developing my original text. What we wanted to do did not work. But it was interesting for me and also for the painter because, even after we discovered that our project would not work, we still maintained our enthusiasm to do something with this idea. And so I have been writing a story out of paintings, using some famous paintings as a source. Fifteen famous paintings would become fifteen different chapters of a novel, a novel that could be the materialization of these paintings through the experience of the narrator.

There is much more communication today than in the past between the intellectuals of North America and those of Latin America. When I was at the university, I remember we read many North American writers. North American literature was very important to us—Faulkner, Hemingway, Dos Passos. At that time their works were what we read, and with enormous enthusiasm; and those writers had a great influence on Latin America. But at the same time few Latin American books were read by English-speaking people or translated into English. This situation has changed considerably during the past twenty or thirty years; and in some cases exactly the reverse is happening—Latin American writers now have influence on young American or European writers. In this sense I am much more optimistic because there is a kind of dialogue between our literatures and between our cultures. This dialogue should be improved, of course; though it is much better than in the past, when Latin Americans only received, when what we produced was totally consumed by ourselves.

Index

Reality, 47, 79, 80, 81, 91, 92,
    110
Reyes, Alfonso, 9
Roa Bastos, Augusto, 25, 40
Rulfo, Juan, 40

Salgari, Emilio, 43
Santa María de Nieva, xi, 58,
    64, 77; Mission of, 65, 66
Sarmiento, Domingo F., 37
Saroyan, William, 2n.2
Sartre, Jean Paul: ideas of, 1; in-
    fluence of, on Vargas Llosa,
    48, 50, 53, 54, 85
Scandinavian myths, 5
Schopenhauer, Arthur, 3
"Secret Miracle, The," 15
Serial novels, 102, 104
Serrano, Pedro, 25
Shapras, 65
Shipibos, 65
Sovereignty, 34
Spanish language, 8, 9
Steinbeck, John, 2n.2
Stevenson, Robert Louis, 6
Storyteller, The, xv, xvi, 36
Sur, 1, 8

Tahuantinsuyo, 27, 29, 30
Tellado, Corín, 116
"Theologians, The" (Borges), 14
Time: narrative concept of, 46,
    47, 48, 93, 97, 99
Time of the Hero, The, x–xi;
    characters in, 51, 52, 54; dia-
    logue in, 101; influence of

Faulkner in, 51; influence of
    Malraux in, 51; influence
    of Sartre in, 48–50; levels of
    narration in, 51–52; sets of
    oppositions in, 53
Tirant lo Blanch, 106
"Tlon, Uqbar, Orbis Tertius"
    (Borges), 14
Trotskyite, 147, 153
Tushía, 71, 72, 78, 83–84. See
    also Fushía

Urakusa, 67
"Utopia of a Tired Man" (Bor-
    ges), 12

Valle Inclán, José María del, 9
Valéry, Paul, 2n.2
Vargas Llosa, Mario: ambition
    of, 64; Collège de France,
    21; and the Communist
    party, 48; his concept of
    fiction, 149, 154; creative
    literature, 49; humor in, 85;
    his method of writing, 44–
    46; personal experience in
    the fiction of, 40, 44, 80,
    86; process of writing in, 39,
    57; relationship with Porras
    Barrenechea, 21, 22, 23;
    scholarship to University of
    Madrid, 44; travel to jungle,
    82, 86, 90; University of
    London, 5; University of San
    Marcos, 21; works of, see
    individual titles

A WRITER'S REALITY

was composed in 10½ on 13 Sabon on Digital Compugraphic equipment
by Metricomp;
with display type in Serif Gothic Bold by Dix Type;
printed by sheet-fed offset on 55-pound, acid-free Odyssey Book Cream White,
and Smyth-sewn and bound over binder's boards in Holliston Roxite B,
with Antique Rainbow endpapers,
by Princeton University Press;
with dust jackets printed in 4 colors by Princeton University Press;
designed by Victoria M. Lane;
and published by

SYRACUSE UNIVERSITY PRESS
SYRACUSE, NEW YORK 13244-5160